CELEBRATION O[F]
North W[ales]

Peter Johnson

First published 1995

ISBN 0 7110 2378 6

Published by Ian Allan Publishing

an imprint of Ian Allan Ltd, Terminal House, Station Approach, Shepperton, Surrey TW17 8AS.
Printed by Ian Allan Printing Ltd, Coombelands House, Coombelands Lane, Addlestone, Surrey KT15 1HY.

Title picture: **Corris Railway No 4 arrived on the Talyllyn in 1951, having been purchased from British Railways for £25.00. In June 1954 it takes water at Dolgoch, looking much as it did on the Corris. At this stage its boiler had been overhauled and the saddletank renewed by the Hunslet Engine Co; the fitting of buffers and additional brasswork would come later.** *M. E. Ware*

This page: **2-6-0 No 6392 leaves Pwllheli with the Up 'Cambrian Coast Express' on 9 June 1960.** *R. J. Blenkinsop*

Front cover: **'Manor' class 4-6-0 No 7800 *Torquay Manor* climbs Borth bank with a train from Aberystwyth in September 1962.** *J. G. Dewing/Colour-Rail (BRW14)*

Back cover, top: **Vale of Rheidol Railway No 7 near Rheidol Falls Halt in June 1955.** *T. B. Owen/Colour-Rail (BRW1296)*

Back cover, bottom: **A Pwllheli train seen passing the Camping Coach at Abererch.** *Norman Gurley*

Contents

BR Standard Class 4 No 75023 seen at Winion Halt with a Ruabon-Barmouth train on 31 August 1964.
Andrew Muckley

Foreword

I came late to Wales, having not visited the Principality at all before July 1971 when I took advantage of a British Rail excursion from the Midlands to Aberystwyth, to ride on the Vale of Rheidol Railway, then British Rail's 'last remaining steam outpost'. Later that year I was a passenger on a chartered train up the Cambrian coast line, visiting the Festiniog Railway, thus riding on a substantial part of the remains of the Cambrian system and two major narrow gauge lines within a short space of time. In the course of these journeys I had pointed out to me other places of narrow gauge significance: Welshpool, Machynlleth, Towyn, and Fairbourne, and noted the evidence of former lines at Van, Kerry, Dinas Mawddwy, Dolgellau, Buttington and Moat Lane.

As a consequence of these excursions I have become heavily involved with the Festiniog Railway and have returned to Wales many times, in the process discovering and enjoying both its railways and the splendour of the countryside through which they run. Because of the Festiniog it was North Wales that I explored most thoroughly; discovering the high speed tracks of the Chester & Holyhead and the sinuous curves of the Conwy Valley, varied later by journeys to Porthmadog. By road I came upon the hidden charms of the Glyn and Tanat Valleys, and Arenig, as well as the more obvious Dyfi, Dulas and Wnion.

It will be seen that whilst I was able to discover the delights of steam on the narrow gauge, I was too late to see traditional steam on the standard gauge — it is something I have had to discover through the photographs of others. It is therefore with pleasure that I present this selection, asking that you share it with me, to celebrate steam in North Wales.

By its very nature it is not possible in this book to cover all aspects of the railways in North Wales; for this reason, and as an aid to further reading, a fairly comprehensive bibliography is included. As we are reviewing the pre-1968 era, a minimalist approach is adopted to post-1968 railway events.

As always I extend my grateful thanks to the photographers, more so on this occasion as I had no pictures of my own to draw upon. In particular Dick Blenkinsop, C. R. L. Coles, Norman Gurley, John Scrace, Tim Shuttleworth and John Stretton valiantly rallied to the call.

Peter Johnson
Leicester
May 1995

Below: **Llanymynech station lay on the Oswestry & Newtown Railway, despite its name, just across the Welsh border, in England; it is included here as it forms a suitable boundary marker. It was the terminus of the Shropshire & Montgomeryshire Railway's line from Shrewsbury (right) and the start of the Llanfyllin branch, off the picture to the left. 'Manor' class 4-6-0 No 7800 *Torquay Manor* pulls in with the 9.45am Whitchurch-Aberystwyth on 28 July 1962.** *L. Sandler*

Introduction

It could easily be said that in North Wales the age of steam is not dead. Thanks mainly to the narrow gauge tourist railways which operate there steam is to be found in abundance. But this book is not about the 1990s, it is about an era which ended in the 1960s, when steam was — except for a brief revival in the late 1980s/early 1990s — extinguished on the main lines.

The area covered in this book is substantially that of the post-1974 counties of Gwynedd and Clwyd, but excluding the industrial areas of eastern Clwyd around Wrexham and with some incursions into Powys and Dyfed in the south and west.

That much of the area lies within the boundaries of the Snowdonia National Park is an indication that scenically the area has much to offer. It is a region well known for, and dominated by, its mountains: notably the mighty Snowdonia range in the northwest, the Clwydian Mountains to the east, Cader Idris to the south, the Cambrian range down the centre; not forgetting the Berwyns, the Rhinogs and the Moelwyns. All of these had an effect on the railways, often limiting the choice of routes and almost leading to an over-abundance of narrow gauge construction.

Such industry as there was in the area mainly evolved from the very rock of the mountains. It

Above left: **Trains from Shrewsbury over the joint line via Buttington Junction brought non-GW locomotive types to Welshpool. Ex-Midland Railway '4F' 0-6-0 No 43757 stands at the water tower, the station off the picture on the left, on 8 September 1951.**
F. W. Shuttleworth

Below: **Welshpool, with a building reflecting its short-lived status as the headquarters of the Oswestry & Newtown Railway, was also, with three through platforms and a bay, the largest intermediate station on the Cambrian's route to the coast. A 'Manor' pauses with a westbound train.**
Ian Allan Library

Note:
Throughout the 20th century the process of returning to Welsh for place names has continued. Except when used in railway company names, current forms are used, even when not contemporary with the period described. Attempts at consistency may not have been successful!

tended to involve mining or quarrying stone, sometimes granite but usually slate, the exploitation of which was to bring about the construction of most of the narrow gauge railways which were to become a feature of the district.

Agriculture usually was, and is, sheep or cattle, with some grass for feed. The land, being founded on rock, is not of high quality but it usually allowed enough to be produced so that markets developed and the numerous small towns that characterise the area built up around them.

The area's popularity with tourists, initially attracted by splendid scenery interrupted by remote imposing castles, predates the railways. It was the capacity of the railways to easily carry ever-increasing numbers of holidaymakers which led to large-scale development of the coastal resorts, especially Prestatyn, Rhyl, Colwyn Bay and Llandudno to the north and Aberystwyth to the west. Other smaller resorts could only aspire to the success and numbers attracted to the larger ones; Cardigan Bay Towyn became Towyn-on-Sea as the Great Western Railway sought to increase the number of visitors. Still in Cardigan Bay, developments by the railway company and private enterprise at Borth and Fairbourne respectively never brought the rewards sought by their developers.

Before the railways the area was considered remote. Members of the English aristocracy and upper classes considered it a great adventure to undertake a grand tour of Wales, much as they undertook grand tours of Europe. The only easy access was via Telford's great trunk road to Holyhead, now known as the A5, built to facilitate the carriage of the Irish Mails (as was the later Chester & Holyhead Railway). Only with the advent of the internal combustion engine and the increase in motor traffic did other roads into and within North Wales come to be improved, and this has mostly been within the last 30 years. Ironically, the greatest Welsh road project of all, the recently completed A55 Expressway, ultimately serves the same purpose as both Telford's road and the Chester & Holyhead Railway.

The geographical features described resulted in a wide range of railways being built. The Chester & Holyhead main line has already been mentioned but there are also the secondary main lines of the Great Western and Cambrian Railways, as well as country branch lines, cross-country routes, numerous narrow gauge lines (both public and industrial); not forgetting that this is also the home of tourist railways which were built long before railway preservation was ever dreamed of. We look at them all in the following pages.

Main Lines

The Cambrian Railways

Arguably the most heroic of the lines in the area are those of the late Cambrian Railways. With taxing gradients over Talerddig, in either direction requiring the best of both locomotives and enginemen, to accommodate the railways to the geography on the route to the coast added nearly 20 miles on to the straight line route from Oswestry to Aberystwyth. Likewise, when one sees the singularly distinctive estuarine bridges over the Dyfi (Dovey), Mawddach, Dwyryd and Glaslyn as well as the Aberdyfi (Aberdovey) Tunnels and the cliffs at Friog, the Cambrian lines never fail to impress, even today. These physically demanding routes, with their impact on motive power specification and consequently, timetabling, especially in steam days, added much to the character of the railway.

The Cambrian lines were actually developed by a string of independent companies which eventually, through amalgamation and take-over, became the Cambrian Railways Company. Most of this Company's empire lay within the area covered by this book, the exceptions being the line southwards from Moat Lane Junction, near Caersws, to Talyllyn Junction, where it formed a bifurcated junction with the Brecon & Merthyr Railway's main line, and the lines from Oswestry, to be the Company's headquarters, to Whitchurch and Wrexham.

The first section to be opened of what was to become the Cambrian main line, was the 14-mile-long Llanidloes & Newtown Railway. When opened in 1859 it was isolated from any other railway until the Oswestry & Newtown Railway opened the following year between Newtown and Abermule, and Oswestry to Pool Quay. As a through route, the railway from Oswestry to Llanidloes came into use in 1861. At what became known as Buttington Junction the Oswestry & Newtown Railway met the Great Western and London & North Western Joint line to Shrewsbury; this was double track thence to Welshpool and accommodated the traffic of both the Oswestry & Newtown and the LNWR. Welshpool Station was built in a suitable manner to house the headquarters of the Oswestry & Newtown Railway.

For the sake of completeness it should be recorded that the Oswestry, Ellesmere & Whitchurch Railway was opened in 1863. The next stage in the development of a route to the

Above left: **Moat Lane was the junction with the Mid-Wales line to South Wales. A Brecon train hauled by 'Dean Goods' 0-6-0 No 2388 is seen there in 1948.** *Real Photos*

Below left: **Abermule looking eastwards in 1948. The line on the right is the Kerry branch.** *Real Photos*

Right: **The double-headed Up 'Cambrian Coast Express' enters Talerddig Station having made the climb from Machynlleth in heavy rain on 30 July 1966. The locomotives are BR Standard Class 4 4-6-0s with a 17-ton axle load.** *A. J. Clarke*

coast came with the opening of the Newtown & Machynlleth Railway in 1863. Between Moat Lane Junction (at first called Caersws Junction but renamed before the Newtown & Machynlleth opening) and Newtown this railway shared the track of the Llanidloes & Newtown Railway.

The 27 miles of the Newtown & Machynlleth Railway included the mighty climbs and cuttings to and through Talerddig. Heading westwards from Newtown, itself 399ft above sea level, Talerddig is reached at 693ft with a steepest gradient of 1 in 71 at 480ft Pontdolgoch. On the west side of the climb the steepest section is slightly more than two miles at 1 in 52 near Llanbrynmair (389ft). Machynlleth is a mere 48ft above sea level.

An Act of 1864 saw the four companies, the Llanidloes & Newtown, Newtown & Machynlleth, Oswestry & Newtown and the Oswestry, Ellesmere & Whitchurch Railways, amalgamated into the Cambrian Railways Co. The Act gave the new company powers to deal with the Great Western, Manchester & Milford and Mid Wales companies, whilst another Act covered agreements with the LNWR.

Meanwhile, since 1861 the Aberystwyth & Welsh Coast Railway had been attempting to build a railway from Machynlleth to the coast and then northwards along the coast to Pwllheli, with a branch to Dolgellau. Machynlleth–Borth was opened in 1863, with Borth–Aberystwyth opening the following year. Along the coast the line was

Left: '**Manor' No 7818** *Granville Manor* **at the head of the 7.55am Birmingham-Aberystwyth starts to descend the Talerddig incline in August 1957.** *Pat Dalton*

Left: **Nearly at the summit of Talerddig, 'Manor' No 7807** *Compton Manor* **hauls the 12.30pm Aberystwyth-Birmingham on 22 August 1959.** *J. Spencer Gilks*

Right: **Almost exactly five years later No 7828** *Odney Manor* **at the same location with the 10.35am Pwllheli-Paddington. The East Lancashire Railway has become the home of No 7828.** *Gerald T. Robinson*

Left: **BR Standard Class 4 No 78006 banks the 10.45am Manchester-Aberystwyth/Barmouth into Talerddig whilst an eastbound pilot waits in the Up loop in August 1959.** *J. Spencer Gilks*

Right: **A 'Manor', No 7807** *Compton Manor*, **heads an eastbound freight near Talerddig during the summer of 1964.** *Andrew Muckley*

opened in sections, not always connected: Aberdyfi–Llwyngwril, with a branch to Aberdyfi Harbour, was opened in 1863; Llwyngwril–Penmaenpool (via what became Barmouth Junction and is now Morfa Mawddach, on the Dolgellau branch) in 1865; Dovey (at first Morben and then Glandovey) Junction–Aberdovey and Barmouth Junction–Pwllheli, with a junction with the LNWR line to Caernarfon at Afon Wen, in 1867; and Penmaenpool–Dolgellau in 1869. The Dyfi, Mawddach, Dwyryd and Glaslyn estuaries, the cliffs at Friog (foothills of Cader Idris) and the tunnels at Aberdyfi combined to make the coast railway difficult to build and operate but with its proximity to the sea, the inland views offered at the estuaries and the castles at Harlech and Criccieth, contributed to it becoming recognised as one of the most scenic routes in the British Isles. The Aberystwyth & Welsh Coast Railway amalgamated with the Cambrian Railways in 1865.

At this stage the Cambrian Railways became a major secondary railway company. Later plans for expansion were invariably thwarted or failed to materialise but it did absorb the Mid Wales Railway in 1904, the Vale of Rheidol Railway in 1913 and the Tanat Valley Railway in 1922. Its locomotive repair shop was established at Oswestry and eventually, in 1901 and 1904, two locomotives were built there.

The Cambrian Railways were absorbed into the Great Western Railway in 1923 and that company made its distinguished mark throughout the region, opening 10 new halts on the coast line in the 1930s where camping coaches also became a feature. The Cambrian survived Nationalisation intact until 1962, when the Mid Wales line from Moat Lane Junction was closed, although Moat Lane–Llandinam remained in use until 1967 for the carriage of materials for the Clywedog dam construction site. Whitchurch–Buttington closed in January 1965 and Aberystwyth–Llanbadarn and Moat Lane–Newtown were singled in 1966. Most of the stations between Welshpool and Aberystwyth were closed in 1965, leaving only six between Shrewsbury and the coast. Apart from Black Rock Halt, closed in 1976, it was only in the 1990s that some of the lesser halts on the Coast line began to be closed.

Left: **Talerddig fireworks. Two BR Standard Class 4s with the 'Cambrian Coast Express' on 27 August 1966.** *W. B. Alexander*

Below: **Ex-GWR '22xx' class 0-6-0 No 2255 required a banker to deal with an Aberystwyth-Oswestry goods near Llanbrynmair on 12 May 1954.** *W. A. Camwell*

Right: **Passengers at Commins Coch Halt wait for BR Standard Class 4 2-6-4T No 80132 to come to a stand with an Aberystwyth-bound local on 31 August 1964.** *Andrew Muckley*

Above: **Cemmaes Road is the location of ex-GWR 2-6-0 No 6378 with the 3.45pm Shrewsbury-Aberystwyth local on 21 August 1959. The Mawddwy Railway terminus was behind the goods shed.** *J. Spencer Gilks*

Below: **The Up 'Cambrian Coast Express', 9.50am from Aberystwyth, has 'Manor' No 7819 *Hinton Manor* in charge as it approaches Cemmaes Road on 31 August 1964.** *Andrew Muckley*

Above: **Complete with 'Cambrian Coast Express' headboard, 'Manor' 4-6-0 No 7823** *Hook Norton Manor* **stands at Machynlleth on 7 July 1962. The locomotive for the Pwllheli portion stands on the left.** *John Scrace*

Below: **After the departure of the Aberystwyth portion of the Cambrian Coast Express '43xx' 2-6-0 No 6395 brings the Pwllheli portion into Machynlleth's down platform on 7 July 1962.** *John Scrace*

The driver of No 82021 keeps an eye on the photographer whilst his locomotive is being turned at Machynlleth in August 1964. *Andrew Muckley*

Above: **No 894 was built by Beyer Peacock for the Cambrian Railways in 1908 and reboilered by the GWR in 1924; it was first numbered 31 then 100 by the Cambrian. It was photographed at Machynlleth on 30 August 1951.** *A. A. G. Delicata*

Below: **No 844 was Cambrian Railways No 15, built by Beyer Peacock in 1918; Judging by the coal in the tender, it had a full day's work in front of it when seen in June 1953. The following year it was being used as a stationary boiler at Oswestry.** *P. B. Whitehouse*

Above: **GWR 'Earl' class 4-4-0 No 9001 was Oswestry-based when seen at Machynlleth in 1948.**
Real Photos

Below: **Machynlleth locomotive shed was built in two stages, that nearest the camera in 1873. The roof was rebuilt by the GWR in 1932, the original being double pitched. 24 locos were allocated here in 1947. Standard Class 2 2-6-0 No 78006 stands alongside an ex-GWR 2-6-2T in June 1960.** *Norman Gurley*

Left: **GWR 'Duke' class 4-4-0 No 328**
Tregenna **makes a fine sight as it takes the Aberystwyth line at Dovey Junction in 1937. The make-up of the train provides additional interest. Dovey Junction had no public road access, although in the 1980s the author saw the signalman's car within 50ft of the signalbox.**
Real Photos

Above: **Aberystwyth shed was noted for the smartness of the locomotives turned out for the 'Cambrian Coast Express'. On a hot day in August 1960 'Manor' No 7818** *Granville Manor* **displays the Aberystwyth style as it heads the Down working near Bow Street.** *J. Reeves*

Left: **The Up 'Cambrian Coast Express' leaves Aberystwyth behind 'Manor' No 7819** *Hinton Manor* **in June 1963.** *Real Photos*

Above: **No 7819 *Hinton Manor* stands in the Carmarthen bay platform at Aberystwyth prior to working the hoppers visible behind it to Oswestry in May 1956. No 7819 is preserved and based on the Severn Valley Railway.**
Pat Dalton

Below: **Cambrian Railways 4-4-0 No 61 became No 1088 under GWR ownership and is seen here, outside Aberystwyth locomotive shed, carrying the GWR number and the Cambrian's livery on the tender. The locomotive was built in 1893 by Sharp Stewart.**
LPC

Left: **Another member of the 'Manor' class preserved is No 7822** *Foxcote Manor*, **owned by the Foxcote Manor Society and based at Llangollen. It is seen on 29 May 1964; Aberystwyth shed is to the right. First established in 1891, the present shed was built in 1938. Some 24 locomotives were allocated here at Nationalisation.** *C. L. Caddy*

Below: **'Manor' No 7828 Odney Manor is pictured on arrival at Aberystwyth with the mail on 13 January 1965; the time is 6.45am.** *Andrew Muckley*

Right: **BR Standard Class 3 2-6-2T No 82021 with the 1.38pm from Dovey Junction to Pwllheli approaches Aberdyfi on 12 July 1962.** *John Scrace*

Below: **A fine early 20th century view of the wharf at Aberdyfi. Whilst most of the wagons are branded for the Cambrian, specimens belonging to the GWR and Joseph Hawkins & Sons (Cannock Old Coppice Colliery) are also identifiable. The wharf sidings were closed in 1964 although the local authority had first sought their closure in 1923!** *George & Sons/author's collection*

Right: **This fine photograph of Cambrian Railways 0-4-2 No 7 *Llanerchydol* is too good to miss out, especially as it is supposed to be located at Aberdyfi c1910, although clearly not at the current station. No 7 was built by Sharp Stewart for the Llanidloes & Newtown Railway in 1860.** *Real Photos*

Left: **With the Harbour branch diverging on the left, '43xx' 2-6-0 No 7336 leaves Aberdyfi with a train for Dovey Junction on 12 July 1962.** *John Scrace*

Centre left: **A different view of the Aberdyfi harbour branch is seen in this portrait of BR Standard Class 3 2-6-2T No 82034 with a pick-up freight photographed on 12 July 1962; its proximity to the beach is indicated by its being partially covered in sand.** *John Scrace*

Below: **With Aberdyfi station in the background 2-6-2T No 5555 and Collett-designed '22xx' 0-6-0 No 2222 approach the end of their journey from Shrewsbury to Tywyn on 30 September 1961. They are hauling the Talyllyn Railway Preservation Society's AGM special from Paddington.** *R. J. Blenkinsop*

Right: **The 3.25pm local passenger from Barmouth to Machynlleth pulls in to Fairbourne with '43xx' 2-6-0 No 6395 in charge on 10 July 1962.** *John Scrace*

Below right: **At Barmouth Junction the ladies stare across the Mawddach estuary in 1956, probably straining for a sight of their train emerging from the tunnel onto Barmouth Bridge. There was a triangle here, with platforms only for coa stal and Barmouth-Ruabon services. Like Dovey Junction, Barmouth Junction, later Morfa Mawddach, was one of that élite group of stations with no public road access.** *Reginald F. Smith*

Above: **A local bound for Dolgellau crosses the famous Barmouth Bridge on 19 July 1962.** *John Scrace*

Left: **The opening portion of Barmouth Bridge frames 'Manor' class 4-6-0 No 7827** *Lydham Manor* **on 24 May 1955. The locomotive is preserved on the Paignton & Dartmouth Steam Railway.** *P. H. Wells*

Right: **The bi-directional Distant signal on Barmouth Bridge, seen in 1958.** *David Ibbotson/ F. W. Shuttleworth collection*

Below: **Barmouth Tunnel seen from the train on 22 July 1961; the locomotive is 'Manor' No 7808 *Cookham Manor*.** *T. A. Chadwick*

Above: **'Manor' class 4-6-0 No 7827 *Lydham Manor* and 'Dukedog' 4-4-0 No 9014 approach Barmouth with the Festiniog Railway Society's AGM special on 30 April 1960.** *R. J. Blenkinsop*

Below: **The 12.45pm Pwllheli-Birkenhead leaves Barmouth on 7 September 1955 with 'Manor' class 4-6-0 No 7807 *Compton Manor* in charge.** *A. J. Buckley*

Above: **Cambrian Railways 2-4-0 No 28 *Mazeppa* approaches Barmouth c1900. No 28 was built to the Oswestry & Newtown Railway's order by Sharp Stewart in 1863.** *Real Photos*

Below: **On 19 July 1962 '43xx' 2-6-0 approaches Barmouth with the Down 'Cambrian Coast Express'.** *John Scrace*

Left: **Arriving at Barmouth with a train for Machynlleth on 20 July 1962 is BR Standard Class 4 4-6-0 No 75020.** *John Scrace*

Left: **GWR 'Barnum' 2-4-0 No 3223 c1930.** *Real Photos*

Left: **North of Barmouth Standard Class 4 No 75024 arrives with the 8.40am Pwllheli-Dovey Junction on 19 July 1962. On the left is '43xx' 2-6-0 No 6335 shunting stock.** *John Scrace*

Above: **No 7807 *Compton Manor* awaits its next duty on 16 May 1955.** *P. H. Wells*

Below: **The classic lines of a GWR pannier tank are seen as No 7405 stands at Barmouth on 19 July 1962.** *John Scrace*

Left: **BR Standard Class 3 2-6-2T No 82034 with goods on 8 July 1962.** *John Scrace*

Left: **Harlech is the location of '22xx' 0-6-0 No 2255, seen with the goods on 18 April 1961.** *R. F. Roberts*

Below: **The overbridge which carries the main road and the Festiniog Railway at Minffordd frames Standard Class 4 2-6-4T No 80099 with vans.** *Norman Gurley*

Above: **The Festiniog Railway receives a load of spent BR ballast at its Minffordd interchange yard during the winter of 1965/66. Standard Class 3 No 82005 shunts the wagons.** *Norman Gurley*

Above right: **A Cambrian Railways '61' class 4-4-0 storms away from Harlech under Great Western ownership.** *Ian Allan Library*

Below: **Another view of No 7827** *Lydham Manor,* **on this occasion with the 6.35am Afon Wen-Barmouth on 23 May 1964. The train has just crossed the Glaslyn estuary and is approaching Minffordd, the interchange with the Festiniog Railway. Clearly the locomotive is in full command of the situation.** *Ron Fisher*

The Great Western Railway

The Great Western Railway's first involvement with the railways in the area covered by this book was in encouraging the development of the Ruabon to Barmouth Junction route. By the time the 1923 Grouping had been completed it was the major player in the south of the area, and in most of South Wales too.

Ruabon to Barmouth Junction and Blaenau Ffestiniog

As the companies which became the Cambrian Railways Co were building their lines westwards to Aberystwyth, competition appeared to the north, culminating in a 55-mile route to the coast at Barmouth from Ruabon. Once again the route was formed by a succession of small companies, the first being the Vale of Llangollen Railway, five-miles long and opened from a junction with the Shrewsbury & Chester Railway south of Ruabon to Llangollen in 1862. Next the Llangollen & Corwen Railway was opened in 1865 (and may soon be reopened throughout by the Llangollen Railway). At Corwen a junction

was formed with the Denbigh, Ruthin & Corwen Railway, itself opened in 1864 and operated by the LNWR. In 1866 the Corwen & Bala Railway was opened to Cynwyd and in 1868 it was opened to Bala. The Bala & Dolgelly Railway ran alongside Llyn Tegid and is partially preserved as a narrow gauge line by the Bala Lake Railway; the line opened in 1868. At Dolgellau, the county town of Merioneth, an end-on junction was formed with the Cambrian and opened in 1869. Supported by the Great Western Railway the companies, except for the Bala & Dolgelly, went on to build the Bala & Festiniog Railway, a tortuous line to Llan Ffestiniog which was opened in 1882 to enable the GWR to tap the Festiniog Railway's monopoly on the slate traffic. After the narrow gauge Festiniog & Blaenau Railway had been converted to standard gauge Bala-Blaenau Ffestiniog was available to traffic in 1883. All of the lines were operated by the Great Western and in 1877 the Bala & Dolgelly was absorbed into it. The larger company's grip on the coast route was confirmed when it absorbed the other companies

Above left: **Pen-y-chain serves the famous Butlin holiday camp and was opened in 1933. The holiday camp traffic endowed it with far more facilities than the location alone warranted but the camp brought much traffic to the line on summer Saturdays for many years. No 3209 pulls away with the 5.30pm Pwllheli-Barmouth on 7 April 1961.** *R. E. James-Robertson*

Left: **'Dukedog' No 9014 pilots a Pwllheli-bound train at Porthmadog in June 1960. Traffic is obviously heavy for, apart from the double-headed passenger train, there is a light engine in the platform and a carriage is stabled outside the goods shed.** *Norman Gurley*

Right: **A Barmouth train stands in Ruabon station on 27 August 1963.** *Andrew Muckley*

Above: **Passengers arriving at Ruabon from Chester or Shrewsbury were faced with a large sign advising that it was the junction for Llangollen, Corwen, Ruthin, Bala, Festinioog (sic), Dolgelley (sic) and Barmouth. Truly Ruabon, the sign being photographed in 1949, was a gateway to Wales.** *Real Photos*

Below: **Ex-LMS 2-6-0 No 46508 enters Trevor with a local train heading westwards on 27 August 1963. Local industry, including bricks and chemicals, provided much of the station's traffic.**
Andrew Muckley

Above: **Llangollen has become the headquarters of the Llangollen Railway. The station, in a prominent position alongside the River Dee, is seen with BR Standard Class 4 4-6-0 No 75021 on 27 August 1963. The International Eisteddfod continues to provide much traffic for the railway each summer.** *Andrew Muckley*

Below: **Carrog is seen on 27 August 1963, with No 75024 heading for Dolgellau entering the station.** *Andrew Muckley*

in 1896; the nominally independent Bala & Festiniog Railway was not finally absorbed until 1910. To boost traffic seven halts were opened between Carrog and Dolgellau in the 1920s and 1930s.

Passenger services survived here until 1964, when flooding closed the Llangollen-Bala section, and the final closure was in 1965. Freight lasted until 1968. At Dolgellau the trackbed has been used as the route of the town's bypass. On the Blaenau branch passenger services ended in January 1960 and freight the following year, the closure being hastened by Liverpool Corporation's desire to build a reservoir, flooding the line in the Tryweryn Valley. The present main road between Bala and Trawsfynydd occupies a short section of the trackbed west of Llyn Celyn but the northernmost part remains in service, serving Trawsfynydd nuclear power station via a link line with the LNWR branch at Blaenau Ffestiniog (the link being built at Liverpool Corporation's expense, on Festiniog Railway trackbed, and completed in 1964). The imposing viaduct over Cwm Prysor remains to provide a substantial reminder to passing motorists of how railway companies would invest in a route through difficult country to serve remote areas in the name of competition, maintaining services and infrastructure long after any hope of profit had been lost.

Below: **With the photographer looking towards the sea, No 75027 takes water at Corwen, the intended ultimate terminus of the Llangollen Railway. Corwen was the junction for Denbigh and the Vale of Clwyd Railway.** *Andrew Muckley*

Right: **No 46508 runs through Llanuwchllyn with a train which appears to consist of a brake van and two locomotive tenders. The ultimate destination of the train is Ruabon. Llanuwchllyn is now the western terminus of the Bala Lake Railway.** *Andrew Muckley*

Right: **Bala Junction, showing a train in the Blaenau Ffestiniog branch platform in 1963, 'Change for Bala' instructed the board on the island platform. Bala remains a popular centre for tourists attracted by water sports on the lake and nearby rivers, the Bala Lake Railway and the scenery.** *Andrew Muckley*

Right: **Only two passengers await the double-headed train piloted by 2-6-0 No 3303 at Wnion Halt in 1949. No 3303 has yet to acquire any indication of the change of ownership from the previous year. Dating from 1933, the Halt was 39 miles from Llangollen Line Junction at Ruabon.** *Real Photos*

Above: **At Penmaenpool the railway ran alongside the Mawddach but it is the mountains to the north which provide a backdrop for the Talyllyn Railway Society's AGM special train on 26 September 1964. The locomotives are** *Lydham Manor* **and No 4555. The train would make uncommon use of Barmouth Junction's platform-less south curve before reaching its destination.** *M. Pope*

Below: **Bala looking towards Blaenau Ffestiniog in 1960. Today only close examination of the site will reveal where the railway once existed, a car park, public convenience, industrial units and a fire station being now located on former railway property.** *Real Photos*

Above: **Trawsfynydd is host to No 7414 with a mixed goods on 12 May 1958. A shed capable of housing a single locomotive was formed as a lean-to attached to the goods shed; it was closed in 1961.** *A. Lillywhite*

Below: **Trawsfynydd Lake Halt was obviously not the busiest; perhaps it is the photographer's wife who looks anxiously for the train. It is near here that the present line from Blaenau Ffestiniog terminates.** *Real Photos*

Above: **Blaenau Ffestiniog Central, the terminus of the branch from Bala, seen with No 5810 in charge of a typical train on 15 August 1953.** *H. C. Casserley*

Below: **The end of the Great Western's Blaenau Ffestiniog branch was marked by a special train from Ruabon organised by the Stephenson Locomotive Society on** **23 January 1961. The crowds turned out to watch and photograph, despite torrential rain, typical of the locality some would say. The Festiniog Railway's tracks to Duffws are still** *in situ* **but it was to be over 20 years before it returned to the town, when the position of the two railways would be reversed to that in the picture.** *R. H. Darlaston*

The Chester & Holyhead Railway

The Chester & Holyhead Railway always was, and is, the railway race track of North Wales as it provided the only substantial multiple-tracked route in the area — a provision made easier by its location on the coastal plain. Built with government support to speed the Irish Mails, the exceptional tubular bridges across the River Conwy and the Menai Strait gave it immediate distinction. The later provision of the first water troughs at Mochdre (near Colwyn Bay) added to its fame.

With an Act obtained in 1844 construction started at the line's eastern end the following year, Saltney Junction to Chester opening in 1846. In 1848 the 60 miles between Chester and Bangor and the isolated 20 miles between Llanfair and

Holyhead, on Anglesey, were opened to public traffic, with the route to Holyhead opened throughout in 1850. These simple statements conceal the great effort which went into constructing the Chester & Holyhead Railway — in particular, for the crossings of the Conwy estuary and the Menai Strait — took time, resources and imagination.

Below: **No 46105 on the 10.50am Euston to Llandudno and Holyhead passing through Shotton on 13 September 1954. The bridge at the rear of the train carries the former Wrexham, Mold & Connah's Quay Railway's line from Buckley Junction to Hawarden.** *S. D. Wainwright*

Above: **Stanier-designed 2-6-0 No 42967 passes through Mostyn with a westbound freight on 28 August 1960.** *J. C. Haydon*

Left: **The photographer caught the smartly turned out 'Jubilee' No 45740** *Munster* **at Prestatyn on 11 June 1962.** *A. Tyson*

Above right: **The Porthmadog portion of the Down 'Welshman' approaches Prestatyn on 16 July 1955.** *S. D. Wainwright*

Below right: **Stanier 4MT 2-6-4T No 42567 hauls the District Engineer's Inspection special back to Bangor, seen passing Rhyl Sands, on 4 September 1963.** *A. W. Martin*

Top: **No 45199 passes through Rhyl with the Holyhead-Chester parcels.** *Kenneth Field*

Above: **Class 5 No 44732 with a Down Llandudno excursion approaching Rhyl on 23 August 1959.** *M. Mensing*

Robert Stephenson was the line's engineer and he devised a scheme for the Menai crossing of a tubular beam, through which the trains would run. His original plan for arched bridges foundered on the Admiralty's insistence on 100ft clearance for sailing ships throughout the length of the spans. Gaining approval for the tubular design it was first implemented on the Conwy crossing as a trial, being completed in 1849. After many trials and tribulations the Menai Bridge was completed the following year, the Up tube opening in March, the Down in October.

As an independent company the Chester & Holyhead Railway was not successful despite having what should have been a lucrative contract with the General Post Office, with the Irish Mails to underpin its common carrier traffic. The opening of a three-mile branch to Llandudno in 1858 came too late to save it and in 1859 the Chester & Holyhead Railway was taken over by the London & North Western Railway. Under LNWR ownership the route was successful and facilities and stations increased and improved. Traffic varied from coal and slate to fish and cattle, not forgetting the tourist trade which was to bring much prosperity throughout North

Wales. To reduce journey time water troughs were introduced at Mochdre in 1860; they were transferred to Aber in 1871 and joined by others at Prestatyn in 1885, and Flint in 1871. By World War 1 most of the line westwards to Llandudno Junction had been quadrupled, such was the level of traffic, and the stations rebuilt at the larger seaside resorts, such as Prestatyn, Rhyl and Colwyn Bay.

Serious retraction on the Chester & Holyhead Railway took place in the 1960s, with station closures as well as reductions in the amount of the quadruple track. A serious incident occurred in 1970 when the Britannia Bridge was so badly damaged by fire that the historic tubes could not be repaired or replaced.

Express passenger services remained steam hauled until 1967, by which time local services had been operated by diesel multiple-units (DMUs) for two years.

Below: **LNWR 2-4-0 No 2002** *Madge* **at Rhyl in 1921.** *Real Photos*

Bottom: **A fine array of locomotives, Nos 40580, 42663 and 41120, on shed at Rhyl in September 1952.** *Real Photos*

Above left: **Approaching Rhyl when returning to Birmingham with a Llandudno excursion on 23 August 1959 is Class 5 No 44920.** *M. Mensing*

Left: **'Britannia' No 70018 *Flying Dutchman* leaves Rhyl with the 11.40 Llandudno-Manchester on 19 May 1966.** *Anthony A. Vickers*

Above: **The same train is seen leaving Colwyn Bay with Class 5 No 45345 on 16 July 1966.** *John White*

Left: **An early afternoon arrival at Colwyn Bay in 1909. On Platform 3 the next departure for Llandudno Junction, Deganwy and Llandudno is awaited.** *Real Photos*

Left: **The famous LNWR survivor, No 3020** *Cornwall* **leaves Colwyn Bay with a Directors' special.** *H. Gordon Tidey/Real Photos*

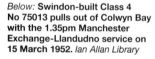

Below: **Swindon-built Class 4 No 75013 pulls out of Colwyn Bay with the 1.35pm Manchester Exchange-Llandudno service on 15 March 1952.** *Ian Allan Library*

Right: **No 45184 approaches Colwyn Bay with a Llandudno-Crewe train on 29 August 1963.** *B. J. Sessions*

Below: **The highly decorated 'Jubilee' No 45647 also carried the cabside stripe to indicate its banishment from under the wires south of Crewe when photographed near Colwyn Bay with the 09.05 Saturdays Only Leeds-Llandudno working on 20 August 1966.** *M. S. Welch*

Left: **'Prince of Wales' class No 2283** *Robert Louis Stevenson* **near Colwyn Bay. The ventilated van is lettered for 'milk and fruit traffic'.**
H. Gordon Tidey/Real Photos

Left: **The Up 'Irish Mail' leaving Colwyn Bay with 'Prince of Wales' class No 2285 in charge.**
H. Gordon Tidey/Real Photos

Below: **Ex-LMS '8F' 2-8-0 No 48253 leaves Llandudno Junction, with ballast from Penmaenmawr, on 7 September 1961.** *Ian G. Holt*

Above: **Class 5 No 44714 approaches Llandudno Junction from the east. The Blaenau Ffestiniog branch joins from the right.** *Ian G. Holt*

Below: **Stranger in the camp: ex-LNER 'B1' No 61165 with the 11.30 Llandudno-Sheffield leaves Llandudno Junction on 25 July 1964.** *P. J. Shirley*

Above: **On a westbound passenger at Llandudno Junction is No 45004 on 18 May 1964.** *F. W. Shuttleworth*

Below: **Locomotives stored at Llandudno Junction on 18 May 1964. Nearest the camera are Nos 84020 and 44525.** *F. W. Shuttleworth*

Above: **Ex-LNWR 0-6-2T No 27618 at Llandudno Junction in 1939.** *Real Photos*

Below: **BR Standard Class 4 No 75010 sets off from Llandudno Junction for Manchester on 8 April 1958.** *G. W. Morrison*

Above left: **A simultaneous departure from Llandudno Junction with an ex-Midland Railway '4P', No 41163, closely followed by a 2-6-4 tank.** *T. W. Gill*

Left: **An Up meat train hauled by No 42982 passes through Conwy Castle walls on 14 June 1962.** *A. Tyson*

Above: **No 42929 heads a Saturday extra out of Conwy** *en route* **for Bangor.** *K. Field*

Left: **With the castle walls behind, BR Standard Class 5 No 73135 approaches Conwy station on 6 Sept 1957. The locomotive had taken over the train, which had originated from Manchester at 11.55am, at Llandudno Junction.** *K. Cook*

Below left: **On 28 May 1966 the 15.10 Manchester-Bangor was one of the few steam workings remaining on the Chester & Holyhead; it is seen passing Penmaen Bach hauled by Caprotti Class 5 No 73130.** *A. Wyn Hobson*

Above: **Over the years the granite quarries at Penmaenmawr have provided a great deal of traffic for the railway. Some of the extensive sidings, complete with loaded wagons, are seen in 1929.** *Real Photos*

Below: **The 3.10pm Manchester-Bangor is seen climbing out of Penmaenmawr on 9 July 1966.** *A. Wyn Hobson*

Left: **An unrebuilt 'Royal Scot', No 6162, emerges from Penmaen Rhos in the 1930s.** *David Ibbotson/collection F. W. Shuttleworth*

Centre left: **'King George V' class No 2271** *J. P. Bickersteth* **with a well-loaded Up train at Aber.** *Real Photos*

Below left: **An LNWR motor train emerges from Llandegai Tunnel in the 1930s.** *David Ibbotson/collection F. W. Shuttleworth*

Above right: **Stanier '8F' No 48632 waits at Bangor's Platform 2 whilst Class 5 No 45280 passes on the midday Holyhead-Broad Street express freight on 7 May 1966.** *A. Wyn Hobson*

Right: **No 40202 with engineering stock at Bangor in June 1960.** *Norman Gurley*

Above: **Empty stock from Caernarfon arrives at Bangor behind Class 5s Nos 44906 and 45069 on 25 June 1966.** *A. Wyn Hobson*

Left: **Class 2 2-6-2T No 41226 arrives at Bangor with a push-pull local from Gaerwen on 3 August 1964.** *M. Dunnett*

bove: **A busy scene at Bangor station yard on 4 December 1965; Standard Class 4 No 75009 is doing the hunting.** *A. Wyn Hobson*

Below: **No 5143 emerges from Bangor Tunnel in the 1930s.** *David Ibbotson/collection F. W. Shuttleworth*

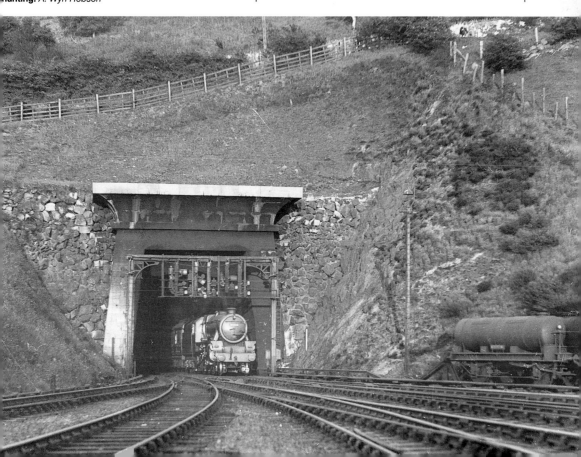

Above: **The Bangor-Amlwch motor train is propelled into Llanfair PG station in August 1964.** *Andrew Muckley*

Below: **Also at Llanfair PG in August 1964, a Holyhead express races through.** *Andrew Muckley*

Right: **No 41200 hauls a mixed goods from Amlwch across the Britannia Bridge in 1949. Despite carrying BR numbers No 41200 is still in LMS livery.** *Real Photos*

Right: **Llanfair PG has achieved fame for having the longest name; it was photographed in 1945.** *Real Photos*

Below: **The full name wasn't always used, as this photograph of motor-fitted No 41224 on a local in 1949 shows.** *Real Photos*

Above: **With steam to spare No 46200 waits to leave Holyhead on 7 August 1961.** *Ian Allan Library*

Below: **No 45531 climbs Holyhead bank on 28 August 1965; the train is the 16.37 Saturdays Only to Euston. A diesel intruder is discernible in the depot behind the train.** *J. Hobbs*

Above: **At the same location a pair of LNWR locomotives wait to leave for the east.** *Real Photos*

Right: **The crew of BR Standard Class 5 4-6-0 No 73043 inspects the train watchers at Deganwy's level crossing; the train is a Manchester-Llandudno express. The locomotive patently has plenty of steam to spare.** *Kenneth Field*

Branch Lines and Independent Railways

Anglesey Central Railway

A branch of the Chester & Holyhead Railway, the Anglesey Central Railway was opened between Gaerwen and Llangefni in 1865 and reached the Amlwch terminus in 1867. The railway was taken over by the LNWR in 1876. Closed to passengers in 1964, the line has remained in use for traffic to a chemical works near Amlwch; proposals for its preservation and the reinstatement of passenger services have been made in the 1990s.

Bangor & Caernarvon Railway

The Bangor & Caernarvon Railway Company built 9½ miles of railway in two sections, both of which opened in 1852: its 8½-mile main line, which left the Chester & Holyhead Railway by a junction at Menai Bridge, and a one-mile branch to Port Dinorwic. The Chester & Holyhead leased the line shortly after it opened and then took it over in 1854, although the Bangor & Carnarvon Railway Company itself was not dissolved until 1867. The line was closed to passengers in 1970 and reopened as a freight terminal until 1972, whilst the Britannia Bridge was being rebuilt; goods services had previously been withdrawn in 1969.

Bethesda and Port Penrhyn

The LNWR'S Bethesda branch connected with the Chester & Holyhead Railway near the eastern end of the Bangor Tunnel. It served the slate quarrying community at Bethesda and was opened in 1884. Passenger services were withdrawn in 1951, although excursions and goods services continued until 1963. The nearby standard gauge branch to Port Penrhyn was owned by the Penrhyn Quarry; it opened in 1852 and closed in 1963. It provided a link between the narrow gauge Penrhyn Quarry Railway and the standard gauge. Ironically, much of the PQR's route was duplicated by the Bethesda branch.

Betws Extension Railway

After reaching Betws-y-coed in 1868, the LNWR decided to build a line onwards to Blaenau Ffestiniog which would compete with the Festiniog Railway. Powers were obtained for a narrow gauge line providing a direct connection with the Festiniog but requiring interchange facilities at Betws-y-coed. Work started in 1872 but the following year it was decided to convert the work to standard gauge, sanctioned as the

Above left: **Motor-fitted No 41226 propels the Amlwch branch train out of Llanfair PG station in August 1964.** *Andrew Muckley*

Below left: **An Amlwch-Gaerwen train pauses at Llangwyllog station in August 1964. The locomotive is No 41226.** *Andrew Muckley*

Right: **No 41226 at Amlwch, freshly arrived from Gaerwen in August 1964.** *Andrew Muckley*

Betws Extension Railway in 1874. Including a tunnel over two miles long, it opened to a temporary platform by the southern tunnel mouth in 1879, and to the permanent Blaenau Ffestiniog station in 1881. To deal with the slate traffic standard gauge transporter wagons and narrow gauge slate wagons were allocated to Blaenau Ffestiniog; these worked to wharves located at Deganwy, on the Llandudno branch. The branch was lengthened in 1982, when services were extended into the platform provided, in the joint station, to accommodate the restored Festiniog Railway. The local freight service was withdrawn from 1987 although for the time being nuclear waste from Trawsfynydd is still carried by rail.

Carnarvon & Llanberis Railway

The eight-mile-long Carnarvon & Llanberis Railway opened in 1869 and was operated by the LNWR from the outset, being jointly owned by it following financial difficulties of the C&L company during construction. The branch was closed in 1964.

Carnarvonshire Railway

The Carnarvonshire Railway was intended to connect Caernarfon with Porthmadog,

Above: **Smoke indicates the recent passage of a train through Blaenau Ffestiniog Tunnel. At slightly over two miles long, the tunnel is the eighth longest in Great Britain. The siding on the left served the Oakeley Quarry, that on the right Greaves's Llechwedd, the line to Blaenau Ffestiniog itself taking the middle route. It will be realised that it was impossible to shunt the sidings without entering the tunnel, much to the Railway Inspectorate's dissatisfaction.** *David Ibbotson*

incorporating part of the Nantlle Railway's trackbed. The coast section between Afon Wen and Porthmadog was eventually built by the Aberystwyth & Welsh Coast Railway. Afon Wen to Caernarfon was opened in 1867 and the line was absorbed by the LNWR in 1870. It was closed in 1964; latterly its heaviest traffic had been generated by Butlin's holiday camp at Pen-y-chain.

Conway & Llanrwst Railway

The Conway & Llanrwst Railway opened in 1863, becoming the first stage of the Conwy Valley branch line south to Blaenau Ffestiniog. Eleven miles long, it made a junction with the Chester & Holyhead Railway east of Llandudno Junction

Right: **The 'Snowdonia' tourist train at Llanberis in June 1960; the locomotive is 2-6-4T No 42611.** *Norman Gurley*

Right: **Llangybi, the second station north from Afon Wen, in August 1964 with No 42075 in charge of a train from Bangor.** *Andrew Muckley*

Right: **Ynys station shows little sign of care or prosperity when seen in August 1964.** *Andrew Muckley*

Above: **Ex-LMS 2-6-2T No 42075 enters Llanwnda with a train for Bangor in August 1964.** *Andrew Muckley*

Below: **'Dinas change here for narrow gauge line' reads the notice on the left-hand platform. The line in question was the North Wales Narrow Gauge Railway, whose terminus lay to the right of the picture. A Holyhead-bound train passes through.** *Author's collection*

Above: **No 42478 with the 'Welshman' approaches Port Dinorwic in June 1960.** *Norman Gurley*

Below: **Midland Railway '1873' class 0-6-0 No 58287 and a brake van are pictured at Denbigh on 23 July 1958. The** imposing station building was designed at the headquarters of the Denbigh, Ruthin & Corwen Railway Co. The signal and post were a replacement, installed within the previous 10 years.
J. A. Peden

and terminated there. The company was taken over by the LNWR in 1867, that company being responsible for the three-mile extension to Betws-y-coed for passengers in 1868.

Denbigh, Ruthin & Corwen Railway

The Denbigh, Ruthin & Corwen Railway linked the Vale of Clwyd and the Llangollen & Corwen Railways, opened throughout in 1864. Before this was achieved there were many machinations as to whether the line, and the Vale of Clwyd, should be controlled by the GWR or the LNWR, the former savouring the prospect of express services to Rhyl from Paddington. The LNWR won and, working the route from 1878, absorbed it the following year. From 1869 there was a junction, north of Denbigh, with the Mold & Denbigh Junction Railway. Passenger services were withdrawn from the Ruthin–Corwen section in 1955 and between Denbigh and Ruthin in 1962; land cruises traversed the complete route until 1961. Freight was withdrawn from Ruthin–Corwen in 1962 and Denbigh–Ruthin in 1965.

Kerry Branch

Less than four miles long, the line to Kerry opened in 1863. It was a branch of the Oswestry & Newtown Railway, leaving the main line at Abermule. At Kerry traffic (the outgoing traffic being timber) was exchanged with the 2ft gauge Kerry tramway, which was run commercially from 1888 to 1895 and under government control from 1917 to 1922. Other traffic consisted of bricks, coal, fertilizer and sheep. Under GW control two halts were opened in 1923 but passengers still lost their service in 1931 — yet another product of the depression. The branch closed in 1956.

Llanfyllin Branch

The railway to Llanfyllin was also a branch of the Oswestry & Newtown Railway and was authorised in the same Act as the Kerry branch, also opening in 1863. It left the O&N at Llanymynech, striking westwards for nearly nine miles before reaching the small market town of Llanfyllin. Much extra traffic was carried in the 1880s during the construction of Vyrnwy reservoirs. The branch closed in 1965.

Left: **Some two miles from Abermule the Kerry branch climbed at 1 in 43 for nearly a mile, the steepest standard gauge gradient operated by Cambrian passenger trains. The top of the incline is clearly seen in this 1948 picture.** *Real Photographs*

Left: **Kerry itself was still a mile away from the branch terminus. The building between the vans was the locomotive shed, long out of use when photographed in 1948.** *Real Photographs*

Above: **Llanfyllin station looking busy on 28 August 1963. No 46512 runs round its train; there is a van outside the goods shed and a wagon in the signalbox siding.** *Andrew Muckley*

Below: **Ex-LMS 2-6-0 No 46512 enters Bryngwyn with a train for Llanymynech on 28 August 1963; for such a location the number of would-be passengers is probably indicative of the rush hour.** *Andrew Muckley*

Above: **Dinas Mawddwy station as it was in 1949, a year before closure. Obviously the branch was not a recipient of the weed-killing train's favours.** *Real Photos*

Left: **The tablet is set down at Bodfari on 27 April 1962.** *Brian Cowlishaw*

Above right: **The Dyserth line passenger services were invariably worked by steam railmotors. No 1, one of three units built by the LNWR in 1905, stands at Rhuddlan Road Halt, near Prestatyn. The photograph was probably taken on one of the first trips with the unit in August 1905.** *Commercial postcard/author's collection*

Below right: **Youthful observers sit on the gate to watch a railmotor set at Meliden, c1920. The siding served lead and zinc mines at Talargoch.** *J. Valentine/author's collection*

Mawddwy Railway

Running northwards from Cemmaes Road, on the Cambrian to the east of Machynlleth, the Mawddwy Railway opened in 1867, its terminus being at Dinas Mawddwy, nearly seven miles further up the Dyfi valley. Traffic was never good and the railway was closed to passengers in 1901 and to freight in 1908, when the line was seriously dilapidated. In 1911 it was reopened as a light railway operated by the Cambrian and in 1923 was absorbed into the GWR. Once again passenger services were the first to be withdrawn, in 1931, whilst freight continued until 1950, official closure taking place the following year.

Mold & Denbigh Junction Railway

Opened in 1869 the Mold & Denbigh Junction Railway was 15 miles long, following a course through the remote valleys of the Clwydian and Halkyn mountains. Always operated by the LNWR, the railway remained independent until 1923, when it became part of the LMS. Closure came on 30 April 1962.

Nantlle Railway

The nine-mile-long 3ft 6in gauge Nantlle Railway was opened in 1828, running from the slate quarries in the Nantlle Vale to Caernarfon, via Penygroes. In 1867 it was taken over by the Carnarvonshire Railway and the Caernarfon–Penygroes section (just over six miles) became part of that company's Afon Wen–Caernarfon standard gauge route. Following the LNWR take-over of the Carnarvon Railway in 1870 the Nantlle Railway was converted to standard gauge from Penygroes to Nantlle village. Less than two miles long, it closed in 1963. The remainder of the line remained horse-worked 3ft 6in gauge and survived to become part of British Railways, also closing in 1963.

Prestatyn & Dyserth Railway

Three miles long, the LNWR-owned Prestatyn & Dyserth Railway opened to serve mines at Meliden and Dyserth in 1869. A passenger service was introduced on the steeply graded

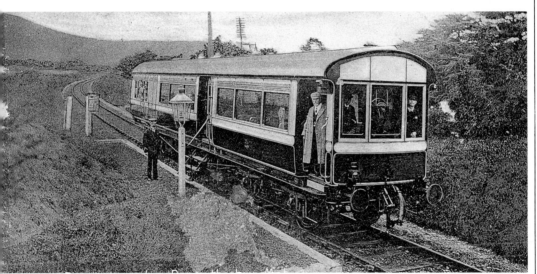

Above left: **It may not be steam but this rare photograph shows the contractor's locomotive used at Llanrhaiadr Mochnant for track lifting during the winter of 1960/1.** *Norman Gurley*

Below left: **The Tanat Valley Railway's Llangedwyn station was untypical of others on the line, being provided with a passing loop, seen here in 1904.** *Real Photos*

Above: **The Van branch platform at Caersws in 1948, eight years after the branch closed. This part of Caersws station remained in use for engineering purposes until the 1970s.** *Real Photographs*

branch in 1905, using steam railmotors initially, and auto trains later. The passenger service was withdrawn in 1930 but the mineral traffic kept the line going until 1973.

Red Wharf Bay Branch

The line to Red Wharf Bay (an area noted for its beaches, which the LNWR hoped would develop as a major tourist resort) started from a junction with the Anglesey Central line at Holland Arms and opened in 1908, to Pentraeth, and 1909, throughout. The branch closed to passengers in 1930 and for goods in 1950.

Tanat Valley Light Railway

Opened in 1904 the Tanat Valley Light Railway ran westwards from a junction with the Cambrian Railways at Porthywaen, terminating at Llangynog, 15 miles away at the foot of the Berwyns. Services were worked by the Cambrian, usually to and from Oswestry. Apart from passengers the traffic consisted of minerals from the quarries around Llangynog, and livestock. Always in debt, the railway passed to the Cambrian in 1921. Passenger trains were withdrawn throughout in 1951; freight was withdrawn between Llangynog and Llanrhaiadr Mochnant in 1952 and completely in 1964.

Vale of Clwyd Railway

The Vale of Clwyd Railway was a branch of the Chester & Holyhead Railway, leaving it at Foryd Junction, west of Rhyl, for Denbigh, 10 miles distant. Opened in 1858 the LNWR worked the line from 1861 and absorbed it in 1867. Trains were worked through to Ruthin, over the incomplete Denbigh, Ruthin & Corwen Railway from 1862. 1955 saw passenger services withdrawn, with freight following suit in 1968.

Van Railway

To serve lead mines near Van the 6½-mile-long Van Railway (leaving the Cambrian at Caersws) opened for goods in 1871 and over two years later it opened for passengers, a service which lasted only until 1879. Following the closure of the lead mines the line closed in 1893. Realising the value of the lead ore as weed-resistant ballast the Cambrian Railways reopened the line in 1896, the quarries reopening at the same time. Despite the quarries closing again in 1920, and being taken over by the GWR in 1923, the railway lasted until 1940.

Narrow Gauge

Bala Lake Railway

Some 45 miles to the south of the Llanberis Lake Railway another lakeside line has been built — the Bala Lake Railway (also on a disused trackbed). The story of the Bala & Dolgelly Railway has been told in the chapter on the Great Western Railway. The narrow gauge line is 1ft 11½in gauge, with its main terminus at Llanuwchllyn, 4½ miles from Bala. It opened in stages between 1972 and 1976. Services are usually operated by former Dinorwic Quarries' Hunslets.

Above left: **Kerr Stewart 0-4-2ST No 4 at Aberllefenni; passengers must board before the train sets off for Machynlleth.** *Loco Pub Co*

Below left: **The two surviving Corris Railway locomotives at Maespoeth shed in April 1948. The shed is now owned by the Corris Railway Society, the locos by the Talyllyn Railway.** *Real Photos*

Below: **No 4 was new in 1921; clearly there is time to spare before it is time to leave for Corris and Aberllefenni.** *Loco Pub Co*

Corris Railway

At 2ft 3in the Corris Railway shared its gauge with the nearby Talyllyn Railway, just as the quarries the railways served shared the same slate veins. Starting life as the Corris, Machynlleth & River Dovey Tramroad, the 11-mile-long Corris opened in 1859, with very little traffic passing to the wharves on the river at Derwenlas after the completion of the standard gauge to Borth in 1863.

The railway was purchased by the Imperial Tramways Co of Bristol in 1878 and three steam locomotives arrived the following year. The Upper Corris branch, which diverged from the main line at Maespoeth Junction, site of the railway's locomotive shed, remained horse-worked, as did the line beyond Aberllefenni, where tramways to several quarries joined. Approval for carriage of passengers was finally obtained in 1883; passenger trains operated between the 6½ miles from Machynlleth to Aberllefenni. A fourth locomotive was bought in 1921. The GWR bought the company in 1930

Above: **Corris No 3 was built by Hughes of Loughborough in 1878; it is seen at Ffrith Wood curve in April 1948.** *Real Photos*

Below: **No 4 crossing the Dyfi. The iron-bodied wagons are lettered to indicate GWR ownership but the locomotive never was given GWR insignia. The far end of the bridge suffered scouring and brought about the railway's closure.** *Real Photos*

and, in common with many of its other branches, withdrew the passenger service in 1931. The Corris Railway was closed within five months of being taken over by British Railways in 1948. The two remaining locomotives as well as some stock were eventually bought for the Talyllyn Railway.

The Corris Railway Society was formed in the 1960s and established a museum in the former Corris Railway stable block at Corris. The Society later acquired the Corris Railway loco shed at Maespoeth and has obtained planning permission for 3½ miles of railway south of Corris.

Right: **Cackler**, built by Hunslet in 1898, seen shunting between the incline foot and the Padarn Railway at Gilfach Ddu on 16 July 1957. It is preserved in Norfolk. *Norman Gurley*

Below: **Maid Marian** was built in 1903 for use on the quarry system's village tramway, hence the domed boiler. At the time of this photograph the original riveted water tank had been replaced. In preservation a cab has been fitted and *Maid Marian* has found a home on the Bala Lake Railway. *Real Photos*

Left: *Cloister* with *Llyn Peris* (left) and *Llyn Padarn* behind; Llanberis is visible on the lakeside, also on **16 July 1957.** *Norman Gurley*

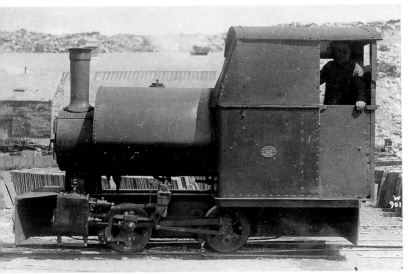

Left: **Dorothea Quarry was in the Nantlle and was first worked around 1829; 2ft gauge steam locomotives were introduced from 1870. The Bagnall** *Wendy,* **seen here, was built in 1919 and arrived at Dorothea in 1930, having first worked at the Votty & Bowydd Quarry in Blaenau Ffestiniog. Becoming disused in the 1940s, it became part of the Hampshire Narrow Gauge collection in 1961. The quarry closed in 1970.** *Real Photos*

Below: **On 16 July 1957 a train of at least 10 wagons loaded with slate waste provide a good load for** *Cloister,* **built in 1891, on the Ponc Fawr level.** *Norman Gurley*

Fairbourne Railway

The two-mile-long Fairbourne Railway started life as a 2ft gauge horse tramway in the 1890s. It was built to aid the development of Fairbourne as a seaside resort, competing with nearby Barmouth. Much of the development was undertaken by McDougall of 'self raising' flour fame. The tramway followed the old road to Penrhyn Point, the embarkation point for ferries across the Mawddach estuary to Barmouth.

As the houses became available for occupation passenger cars were introduced on the tramway, as it ceased to carry materials when building finished. In 1916 the line was taken over by Narrow Gauge Railways Ltd (then owner of the Ravenglass & Eskdale Railway) which, in conjunction with Bassett Lowke, the Northampton model builder, converted it to 15in gauge and introduced steam traction. In this form the railway continued through two changes of ownership until World War 2.

After the war the line was in a severely damaged state and unfit for use. Ownership changed again and it was rebuilt, opening throughout in 1947. Increased passenger traffic encouraged the owners to make a considerable investment in new locomotives and rolling stock.

As much of the line runs along the dunes it is very much at the mercy of the sea and shifting sand. By the 1970s the seaward terminal had ceased to be readily accessible from the beach used by the ferries so a deviation line was built to overcome this problem, taking the line to the landward side of the point, this section coming into use in 1976. Its first passenger use was actually on 22 May that year, a non-service day but the same day that the Talyllyn Railway opened its Nant Gwernol extension so a railtour party from Leicester managed to ride on two new narrow gauge lines on one day!

In 1984 the Railway changed hands again, bringing new owners who regauged the track to 12¼in gauge and realigned the route (including construction of a tunnel) at the point. At the point the new route again takes the line seawards, joining up with the old line at the station and giving the appearance of a terminal loop, as at Dungeness on the Romney, Hythe & Dymchurch Light Railway, but here the engines run-round at the station and trains leave in the same direction as they arrived.

To work the regauged railway four steam engines built in England in 1978/9 for a French line were provided; they were half-sized replicas of prototypes from the Lynton & Barnstaple, North Wales Narrow Gauge, Leek & Manifold and the Himalaya-Darjeeling narrow gauge railways. From 1988 the line has been known as the Fairbourne & Barmouth Railway.

Below: **The Fairbourne Railway's Bassett Lowke 4-4-0 *Count Louis* leaves Fairbourne in July 1934. The locomotive has been displayed at the Birmingham Railway Museum since 1987.** *Real Photos*

Above: *Count Louis* **leaves the Ferry terminus for Fairbourne in the summer of 1953. Behind, a goods train is crossing the famous Barmouth Bridge.** *M. E Ware*

Below: **2-4-2** *Siân* **was built for the Fairbourne Railway by Guest Engineering in 1963 and is seen in the dunes typical of much of the railway's route in September 1968.** *Siân* **has recently spent time on the Bure Valley Railway in Norfolk and in 1995 on the Cleethorpes Coast Light Railway.** *John R. Hume*

Festiniog Railway

The Festiniog Railway Company opened its line between Porthmadog and Blaenau Ffestiniog in 1836. It was built to carry slate from the quarries at Blaenau Ffestiniog to the harbour at Porthmadog, a distance of just over 14 miles (including branches at Blaenau). A narrow gauge of 1ft 11½in was adopted and the railway was designed to have a continuous falling gradient down to the harbour so that laden trains could be worked down by gravity; horses pulled the empty wagons back up the hill. The last mile to Porthmadog (then Port Madoc) utilised Madocks's 1811 embankment across the Glaslyn estuary.

The demand for slate in the developing industrial areas of England and elsewhere brought much traffic to the railway, which was soon operating to capacity. To overcome the difficulties, and to reduce costs, steam locomotives were introduced in 1863. Initially there were four 0-4-0 tank engines, followed in 1867 by two similar, but larger, machines. Greatly rebuilt and modified, four of them still survive, two in working order.

The introduction of steam engines led the way to the (official) carriage of passengers from 1865, a move encouraged by the threat of competing routes to Blaenau Ffestiniog.

The solution to the repeated problem of increasing traffic and limited capacity was *Little Wonder*, an articulated locomotive built to Robert Fairlie's patent. Delivered in 1869, it was fitted with a double-ended boiler unit having twin fireboxes in the middle. *Little Wonder* proved to be very successful and the double Fairlie became the Festiniog's trademark.

With the arrival of the 20th century the FR was to enter a period of decline which was to end, in 1946, in closure and abandonment. The decline was caused both by the tapping of the Blaenau slate traffic by the LNWR (from 1881) and the GWR (from 1883) and the development of alternative roofing materials.

In 1934 the FR took a lease on the Welsh Highland Railway and operated a summer service during the following three years, though with no success, that line closed at the end of the 1936 season.

The FR passenger service was withdrawn on the outbreak of war in 1939, slate trains continuing to run as required and when motive power was available. After the war it quickly became clear that there were no resources, either within the railway or elsewhere, to repair the track and rolling stock so in 1946 the Festiniog Railway was closed.

Almost immediately attempts were made to find ways of reopening the railway, possibly using volunteers to assist a nucleus of paid staff. Eight years were to pass before all the legal and financial obstacles were overcome. Supported by the newly formed Festiniog Railway Society, the railway reopened in stages, Blaenau Ffestiniog being regained in 1982, 150 years since the railway's first Act of Parliament gained Royal Assent.

The section between Dduallt and Tanygrisiau was reopened only after a new route, (including a spiral and tunnel) was built to avoid the lower lake of the CEGB's pumped storage power station at Tanygrisiau. The power station was planned during the closure and in the 1950s the authorities could not be persuaded that a preserved railway was a worthwhile thing. The hundreds of thousands of passengers who have travelled on the Festiniog Railway since it reopened have proved them wrong many times over.

Left: **Tan-y-bwlch has always been the busiest of the Festiniog Railway's intermediate stations, as well as being the largest. From 1958 until 1968 it was the railway's terminus, too, and is seen on 14 July 1962, apart from the cars, much as it was before the railway closed. The locomotive is** *Earl of Merioneth,* **previously** *Taliesin* **and originally** *Livingston Thompson.* *John Scrace*

Below left: **Merddin Emrys was the first Fairlie built at Boston Lodge, in 1879. It is seen at Clogwyn Daniel in the 1930s. The trackbed here forms part of the access road to the Tanygrisiau pumped-storage power station and the area to the right is flooded by Llyn Ystradau.** *R. Piercy*

Above right: **Taliesin shunts carriages at Harbour station in the 1930s. Built at Boston Lodge in 1886, the name** *Taliesin* **was applied when the locomotive returned to traffic after an overhaul completed in 1931.** *Real Photos*

Right: **Steam locomotives taking water invariably provide scope for photography and examination;** *Merddin Emrys* **is both replenished and scrutinised in 1936. The body of four-wheeled carriage No 11 was built by Ashbury in 1868, Boston Lodge providing the running gear; it seated 12 and no longer exists.** *C. R. L. Coles*

Below: **A portrait of** *Taliesin* **coming to a stand at Harbour station in 1936.** *C. R. L. Coles*

Left: Penrhyn station was the Festiniog's terminus in 1957. On 23 November that year General Manager Allan Garraway and a local child look on as *Prince's* fireman rummages around the tender's toolbox. *G. E. Baddeley*

Left: Prince tackles the climb out of Minffordd Yard with loaded slate wagons in the 1950s. The railway claims that 1863-built *Prince* is the oldest steam locomotive in regular use in the world. *Author's collection*

Below: In 1901 the crew of one of the England engines pose for the camera with their unusual train standing on the Up line at Tan-y-bwlch, the wrong line for the direction of travel. A chain is attached to the tender to allow uncoupling on the move. A gunpowder van, one of the FR's few private-owner wagons and presumably empty, is marshalled next to the loco. *Real Photos*

Right: Palmerston was on its last legs when photographed in 1934; the firebox dated from 1909 and the boiler barrel from 1904, the latter having previously seen service in *Little Giant* until 1932. From 1940 *Palmerston* provided steam for a steam hammer at Boston Lodge. *Real Photos*

Right: The Penrhyn Quarry Railway's *Linda* was obtained by the FR on loan in 1962. It is seen as received, with a train of coal wagons on the mineral line at Minffordd. *Author's collection*

Below: Blanche and *Linda* were bought in 1963. The former is seen passing Pen Cob, at the Merioneth end of Maddocks's Cob, on 3 August 1965, shortly after receiving its tender-cab. At this time Pen Cob was a popular request stop for users of the nearby beach; now the sand has become grassed-over mud and unattractive to all except the occasional sheep. *G. W. Shott*

Festiniog & Blaenau Railway

Opened in 1868 the Festiniog & Blaenau Railway shared its gauge with the Festiniog Railway and made a junction with that railway at Blaenau Ffestiniog. 3½ miles long, it served the quarrymen who lived at Llan Ffestiniog and the Manod and Craig Ddu slate quarries. The line's most notable feature was a timber viaduct at Tan-y-Manod. The railway was absorbed by the Bala & Festiniog Railway in 1883 and converted to standard gauge, the viaduct being rebuilt in stone.

Above: **One of the Festiniog & Blaenau Railway's Manning Wardle 0-4-2STs, built in 1868; they remained in service until the Great Western completed the gauge conversion in 1883. The location of the photograph is uncertain but it could be at Llan Ffestiniog.** *Real Photos*

Below: **The timber viaduct at Tan-y-manod in the 1870s; the viaduct was replaced by a stone structure when the line was converted to standard gauge.** *John Thomas*

Glyn Valley Tramway

Probably the strangest of the lines featured in this book, the Glyn Valley Tramway had a gauge of 2ft 4½in and was eight miles long, the running line extending from Chirk to Glyn Ceiriog. It opened in 1873, for freight (mainly slate and granite) and in 1874 for passengers. Despite being a roadside tramway it was at first a gravity line, horses dealing with the empties on the uphill journeys. In 1888 the first of three Beyer Peacock 0-4-2 tram engines arrived, the second following in 1889 and the third in 1892. An ex-military Baldwin 4-6-0T was obtained in 1921. The passenger service was lost in 1933 and the line closed completely in 1935. Two of the carriages were rescued and are used on the Talyllyn Railway.

Above: **Glyn Valley Tramway No 3** *Glyn* was ordered from Beyer Peacock in 1891 and delivered the following year; it was the only GVT engine to be numbered and was 12in longer than its predecessors. It was around four years old when photographed at Glyn Ceiriog. *Real Photos*

Right: Although ordered for the Portmadoc, Beddgelert & South Snowdon Railway, and named after its receiver, *Russell* was delivered to the North Wales Narrow Gauge Railways. It is seen at Dinas before World War 1 with the single Fairlie *Gowrie*; possibly the latter, built 1908, has just been delivered for it has no name plates. *Real Photos*

The Padarn Railway

The Padarn Railway, the Dinorwic Quarry Railway, was a 4ft gauge 6½-mile-long line brought into use in 1843 to replace an earlier tramway. It was built to convey the output of the Dinorwic slate quarries, just outside Llanberis, to the quarry-owned Port Dinorwic, on the Menai Strait. Horse-worked at first, locomotives were introduced in 1848 when two 0-4-0s were obtained from A. Horlock's Northfleet Ironworks in Kent. In 1882 and 1886 they were replaced by Hunslet 0-6-0Ts. A third Hunslet was added to the fleet in 1895.

Padarn Railway operations were unusual in that the 1ft 10¾in gauge quarry wagons were carried, loaded, to the port on 4ft gauge transporter wagons. No public service was offered, but from 1895 until 1947 trains were run for the benefit of the quarrymen.

In the quarries the different levels were served by 1ft 10¾in gauge systems. Locomotives were used where the length of run or the amount of work warranted it; otherwise manpower was used. Most of the tracks at Port Dinorwic were of the narrower gauge and engines were allocated there for shunting purposes. From 1870, 29 steam engines and a smaller number of internal combustion locomotives were used at varying times. The quarry workshops at Gilfach Ddu carried out running repairs to the locomotives; major repairs and rebuilds were carried out at the port by the Port Dinorwic Dry Dock Company, a linked organisation.

The Padarn Railway was closed in October 1961. The quarries followed in 1969 when the company went into liquidation — much of the site is now that of PowerGen's Dinorwic Power Station — a pumped storage station much larger than the prototype which resulted in the Festiniog Railway's deviation being built. Whilst most of the Padarn Railway's equipment was scrapped this was not to be the fate of the quarry railway equipment, much of it surviving in Wales and elsewhere. Two miles of the Padarn Railway route was reopened from Gilfach Ddu as the Llanberis Lake Railway in 1971/2. The gauge of the new line is 1ft 11½in and the three locomotives owned by the operating company are Hunslet 0-4-0STs from the Dinorwic Quarries. The former quarry workshops at Gilfach Ddu are preserved and opened to the public; ex-Penyrorsedd Quarry Hunslet 0-4-0ST *Una* is to be found there, occasionally in steam.

Left: The tram engines' wheel arrangement was 0-4-2 and they usually ran cab leading. Both types of carriage in the photograph were designated third class and were built by the Midland Railway Carriage & Wagon Co, seating 16 passengers. The open cars were for the tourist traffic. On this occasion the train has been run into the coal yard at Glyn Ceiriog. *R. E. Tustin collection*

Above right: The Hunslet Locomotive Co built *Amalthea* in Leeds in 1886, the second of this type constructed for the Padarn Railway. Named *Pandora* at first, the engine was renamed in 1909. The railway ceased operating in 1961 and *Amalthea* was cut up two years later, the photograph taken in June 1960. *Norman Gurley*

Right: Velinheli was built in 1895; it was paid for by the quarrymen for it was intended to haul their works trains, but that didn't stop the quarry management using it to haul slate! One of the 4ft gauge transporter wagons can be seen carrying a loaded 1ft 10in gauge wagon behind. *Real Photos*

Below: The third of the Padarn Railway's Hunslets, Dinorwic, makes a good start from Gilfach Ddu on 1 April 1959. For many years the shed behind the locomotive was home to Fire Queen. This section of the trackbed is now occupied by the Llanberis Lake Railway. *J. A. Peden*

Above: **Port Dinorwic in 1948. Amongst the dockside clutter can be discerned a traction engine and a vertical boiler as well as the mast of a ship in the dock. The sidings were a branch of the LNWR and the buildings the ship repair shops.**
Real Photos

Above right: **New to the Penrhyn Quarries in 1899 the Hunslet *Nesta* was one of six Penrhyn locos sold to the US in 1965 and was last reported in Georgia. The**

photographer recalls a climb of over 2,000ft to take the photograph on 15 July 1957. *Norman Gurley*

Below right: **Built by Barclay in 1931, *Glyder* was first used on the Durham County Water Board's Burnhope Reservoir construction until purchased by Penrhyn in 1938. Photographed in June 1960, *Glyder* travelled with *Nesta* to North America in 1965 and is reported to be at the Early Wheels Museum in Indiana with *Ogwen* and *Winifred*.**
Norman Gurley

Penrhyn Quarry Railway

The six-mile-long Penrhyn Quarry Railway was another private line built for the carriage of slate from the Penrhyn Quarries, near Bethesda, down to Port Penrhyn on the Menai Strait. Over the course of time there were three railways which performed this duty, the oldest opened in 1802 (the first narrow gauge railway in North Wales). The most recent Penrhyn line was built in the 1870s to 1ft 10¾in gauge. As with the Dinorwic, the only official passengers were the quarrymen. The railway was steam-worked from the start, with de Winton locomotives being used initially. In 1882 the Hunslet 0-4-0ST *Charles* was obtained, followed by the similar *Linda* and *Blanche* in 1893. These locomotives proved well suited to the line and were in regular use until the line closed in 1962. *Blanche* and *Linda* and substantial amounts of track materials were transferred to the Festiniog Railway, where all continue to give good service. Also as at Dinorwic, the Penrhyn Quarries had extensive rail systems throughout the quarries, much of them worked by locomotives which have been preserved. Despite the closure of the railway, the quarries continue in production under changed ownership.

Left: Winifred was delivered from Hunslet in 1885; it is seen with a train of slate waste on 24 August 1962. The wagons alongside contain dressed slate. *Norman Gurley*

Below left: Penrhyn Quarry locos started to fall out of use in the 1940s and the line of derelict engines which accumulated outside the Coed-y-parc workshops until disposals started in the 1960s became a focal point for visiting enthusiasts. The collection of disused locomotives is seen on 24 August 1962. *Norman Gurley*

Above right: Lilla was one of a number of second-hand locomotives obtained by Penrhyn in the 1920s and 1930s. It was built by Hunslet in 1891 for the Cilgwyn slate quarry and transferred to Penrhyn, travelling over part of the Welsh Highland Railway to do so, in 1928. Larger than most of the other quarry locos, *Lilla* was intended for use on the main line but spent most of its time on Red Lion level, where it was photographed in 1950. Out of use in 1957, it was sold to Bernard Latham in 1963 and since 1993 it has been on the Festiniog Railway. *Real Photos*

Centre right: The first locomotives used on the Penrhyn Quarry Railway were built by de Winton in Caernarfon. They started to be replaced from 1882 when *Charles* was delivered from the Hunslet Engine Co. Worked for the last time in 1958, *Charles* passed to the National Trust in 1963, being displayed at the Penrhyn Castle Museum. In 1951 it was photographed outside the Coed-y-parc workshops. *Real Photos*

Below right: With a train of loaded rubbish wagons *Edward Sholto* was photographed in 1951. Built in 1909, the locomotive was out of use from 1956, sold to Canada in 1960 and was last reported in Illinois, USA. *Real Photos*

Left: In 1893 the railway acquired *Linda* and *Blanche*. The latter is seen leaving Port Penrhyn with a train of slate empties on 15 July 1957. The bucket carried sand in case of greasy rails. *Norman Gurley*

Below: *Blanche* and *Winifred* at Port Penrhyn in 1947, the photograph showing the family resemblance in the different types of locomotives. *Real Photos*

Right: **Pendyffryn** was built for the Penyrorsedd Slate Quarry by de Winton in 1894. The chimney extension aids steam raising. Seen c1932, *Pendyffryn* was out of use in 1949 and sold in 1965, being presently in store on the Brecon Mountain Railway.
W. H. Whitworth/Real Photos

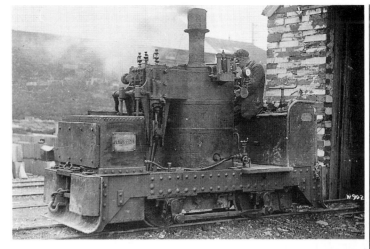

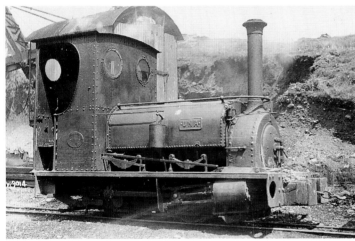

Left: **Una** was the last of three Hunslets built for Penyrorsedd between 1899 and 1905. From 1977 it has been on display at the Welsh Slate Centre at Llanberis where it is steamed from time to time. *Real Photos*

Right: Seen in June 1960, *Diana* was a Kerr Stewart built in 1917. When new it worked at the sawmills served by the Kerry branch. It transferred to the Oakeley Slate Quarry in Blaenau Ffestiniog in 1925 and was sold to a dealer in 1942, reaching the Penyrorsedd in 1945. Probably very little used there, since 1976 it has been stored at the Brecon Mountain Railway. *Norman Gurley*

Left: **The Portmadoc, Beddgelert & South Snowdon Railway was an early 20th century scheme to connect the North Wales Narrow Gauge Railway to the Croesor Tramway, that is to create the Welsh Highland Railway some 20 years earlier than was eventually to be the case. Some work was done, which may still be seen, in the Beddgelert area around 1906 and the locomotive *Russell* was ordered. The photograph shows abandoned formation and track at Pitts Head in 1920.** *Real Photos*

45747. MINIATURE RAILWAY, RHYL PLEASURE PARK, RHYL.

Left: **The 15in gauge railway around the marine lake at Rhyl was opened in 1911, using two Bassett-Lowke locomotives. One of them is seen here, near the turnout to the locomotive shed. The LNWR main line is behind the wall.** *The Photochrom Co/commercial postcard*

Below: **From 1920 a series of six Greenly-designed 4-4-2 locomotives were built at Rhyl; one of them, *John* or *Joan*, is seen in the 1920s.** *Commercial postcard*

Snowdon Mountain Railway

The Snowdon Mountain Railway is a Swiss mountain railway transposed to North Wales. The mountain is the highest peak in England and Wales; the railway on it was the first of those described in this book to be built exclusively for its current traffic — tourists.

The railway is a rack line built to the 'Abt' principle and construction started in December 1894. Whilst carriages, wagons and track materials were ordered from English firms, three steam locomotives were ordered from Switzerland, the centre of mountain railway expertise. The finished railway was 800mm (2ft 7½in) gauge and 4½ miles long with a ruling gradient of 1 in 5½.

The official opening took place on Easter Monday, 1896. An accident on the first day caused services to be suspended while investigations were carried out; the railway was reopened to the public on 19 April 1897. By this time the company owned five locomotives although the remains of one of them were in an irrecoverable location on the mountainside. They were built by Schwezierische Locomotiv-und Maschinenfabrik at Winterthür, Switzerland, and have the appearance of being 0-4-2Ts with inclined boilers.

By the 1920s the railway was sufficiently well-off to buy additional rolling stock from Switzerland: three new locomotives and four new carriages. Unlike many other organisations, the SMR made profits during the 1930s and entered World War 2 in good order. During the war the summit buildings were taken over by different sections of the armed forces and many trains were operated On His Majesty's Service.

After the war public services were resumed in 1946. From 1956 a programme of locomotive overhauls was commenced, the four eldest being sent away, one each year from 1958, for the work to be carried out; work on the others, including firebox replacement, was undertaken at Llanberis and this is the current practice. The track was relaid throughout from 1967.

Capital from a share issue was used to finance the construction of two Hunslet diesel locomotives delivered in 1986. To supplement the diesels a new carriage was delivered from East Lancs Coach Builders Ltd in 1988. Two further diesel locomotives were obtained in 1991 and 1992.

Below: **A typical Snowdon ensemble approaching the summit.** *Real Photos*

Left: **Named for the mountain, No 4 stands at Llanberis showing how the boiler is inclined in order to cope with the railway's gradients.** *H. Thompson*

Right: **Most maintenance of SMR locomotives is carried out in the Llanberis running shed so occasionally locos are shunted into the open in a dismantled state. One of the older engines so emerged c1932.** *W. H. Whitworth/Real Photos*

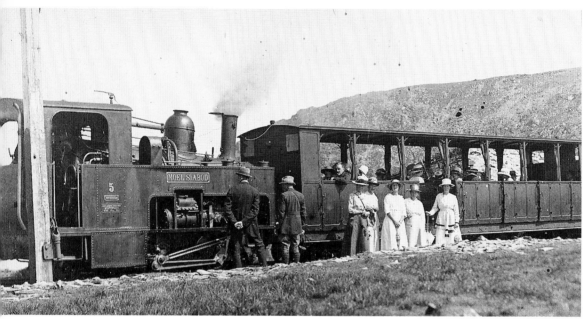

Above: **No 5 *Moel Siabod*, built 1896, at Clogwyn in 1907.** *H. Gordon Tidey/Real Photos*

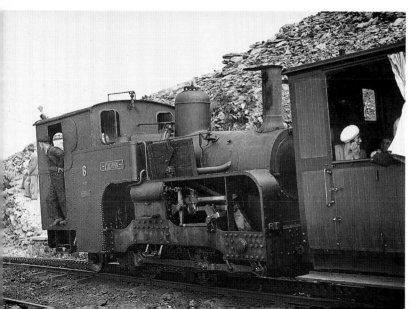

Left: **The driver of No 6 and the pedestrians behind look out for a second train arriving at the summit. The locomotive was built in 1922, the tanks carrying 374gal compared to the 525gal of Nos 7 and 8 supplied the following year.** *Real Photos*

Talyllyn Railway

The 2ft 3in gauge Talyllyn Railway was opened in 1866. Just over six miles long, it was designed to carry slate from the Bryn Eglwys quarries to a wharf adjacent to the Cambrian Railways' coast line at Towyn, in the old county of Merioneth. The railway company, established by an 1865 Act of Parliament, was a wholly owned subsidiary of the Aberdovey Slate Co, then recently formed to quarry the slate as a diversion from the depressed Manchester cotton trade, itself affected by the American Civil War.

The line runs along the southern valley side of the Afon Fathew, opposite the mass of the Cader Idris range. The statutory Talyllyn Railway terminated at a spot some half a mile from the village whose name it bears; access to the quarries was by a branch line three quarters of a mile long, which made an end-on connection to the main line through a series of inclines. On opening, the minimum of equipment was provided: two locomotives called *Talyllyn* and *Dolgoch*, three four-wheel carriages and a fleet of wagons. With the addition of a further carriage this stock sufficed for the Talyllyn Railway for over 80 years.

Wharf station, the coastal terminus, was for goods only, passengers being accommodated at Pendre, on the edge of the town. Pendre was also the location of the railway's stock sheds. The main intermediate station became Dolgoch, where a locomotive water supply was laid on, close to a fine three-arch viaduct, 62ft high and the line's only major structure, by which it crossed a ravine. Until 1976 Abergynolwyn was the inland passenger terminus. Goods traffic did reach the village by rail, however, as a branch off the mineral line, which included a cable-worked incline, served a goods shed, a sawmill, the

Railway Hotel, as well as two terraces of houses.

The local MP, Sir Henry Haydn Jones, took over the quarries and the railway in 1911 and managed to keep the railway going until he died on 2 July 1950; his executors running it until the end of that season. (The remaining working quarry had closed after the roof collapsed in 1946.)

In 1950 there were no preserved railways and the idea of amateurs involving themselves in railway operation was completely alien to both enthusiasts and the public. Already, attempts to reopen the Festiniog Railway with the aid of volunteers had been unsuccessful.

However, following Sir Henry's death enthusiasts decided to form a preservation society and to approach the executors of the Haydn Jones estate. Following negotiations it was agreed to form a new company, in which both parties would be represented, to hold the TR shares. In this way

Above: **From its opening in 1866 until 1951 the Talyllyn Railway made do with only two engines, the older being No 1 *Talyllyn* shown here at Wharf station in the 1930s.** R. E. Tustin

105

the first railway preservation society was formed and with its support the Talyllyn Railway reopened for business in 1951, although with services terminating initially at Rhydyronnen due to poor track condition.

In addition to running the trains, the new society undertook to search for new equipment so that the 1866 stock could be repaired and augmented. Two locomotives and some rolling stock previously used on the Corris Railway were bought from British Railways; on the Talyllyn the locomotives became No 3 *Sir Haydn*, the previous owner, and No 4 *Edward Thomas*, the line's manager for many years.

Following several years of hard work, mainly undertaken by volunteers, services were extended to Nant Gwernol, using the mineral extension trackbed, in 1976.

In 1969 the railway obtained a 3ft gauge Barclay 0-4-2T from the Bord Na Mona, the Irish Peat Board. The locomotive, built in 1949, had seen little use and it was proposed to convert it to work on the TR. Using major components as the foundation, a new locomotive, No 7 *Tom Rolt*, named after the Society's founder, entered service in 1990, the year in which the railway celebrated its 125th anniversary and the preservation society its 40th.

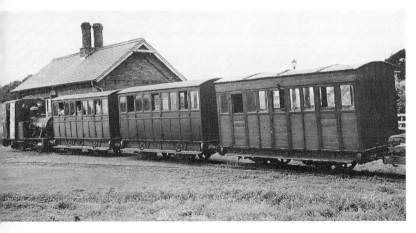

Above: **Brynglas is the location of this** *Dolgoch*-**hauled Talyllyn train seen on a wet day in 1949. Perhaps the open door of the first carriage indicates where the photographer was travelling.** *Real Photos*

Left: **No 2** *Dolgoch* **arrives at Wharf with slate wagons bringing up the rear. The carriages nearer the locomotive were built by Brown Marshalls & Co Ltd, the third by the Lancaster Wagon Co Ltd. There are no doors on this side, all the railway's platforms being located on the same side of the track. For stopping the train is dependent on the locomotive and any braked slate wagons.** *Raphael Tuck & Sons Ltd/commercial postcard*

Right: **With passengers on board, No 2 runs up to the water tower on the mineral extension at Abergynolwyn.** *P. B. Whitehouse*

Right: **Named** *Edward Thomas* **after the line's last pre-preservation manager, TR No 4 attracts a good crowd of admirers as it runs round at Abergynolwyn.** *Norman Gurley*

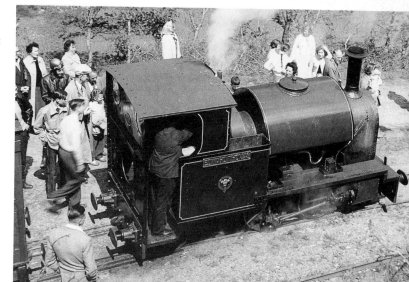

Right: **In 1958 the railway accepted an offer to fit No 4 with a Giesel ejector, in which form it ran until 1969. The 3pm departure from Tywyn leaves Rhydyronnen on 28 July 1967.** *Allan Stewart*

Above: 1950s. Still neither locomotive has buffers, standard on the TR, but No 4 has started to acquire additional brasswork. No 3 operated chimney-first down hill at this time, due to problems with crew access caused by the positioning of the vacuum brake equipment. *Ian Allan Library*

Below: No 6 *Douglas* was donated to the Talyllyn Railway by a contractor in 1953. It is seen preparing to leave Tywyn on 17 July 1962, with a train including vehicles from the Corris and Penrhyn Quarry Railways and the Glyn Valley Tramway. *John Scrace*

Above: **No 2 *Dolgoch* at Pendre with the 4.10pm ex-Wharf on 24 August 1964. A carriage shed was later built on the land behind the train. The first two vehicles behind the loco both originate from the Corris Railway.**
A. W. Martin

Below: **One of the unusual features of the 'old' Talyllyn Railway was the incline connected to the mineral extension to serve Abergynolwyn village itself. Ingoing loads included coal and beer, whilst the outgoing was usually night soil. One of the incline wagons seen in this 1903 picture has recently been restored for inclusion in the railway's vintage goods train.** *H. Fayle/Real Photos*

On the Vale of Rheidol Light Railway Nos 7 and 9 with the 1.45pm and 2.30pm Aberystwyth departures on 1 August 1960. *J. J. Davies*

Vale of Rheidol Light Railway

At the end of the 19th century the Rheidol valley, near Aberystwyth, was a hive of industrial activity. The various metal mines in the area were in increasing need of improved communications between them and the port (and growing resort) of Aberystwyth. The miners, and others, had to continue using the poor quality road network with pack animals until 1902, when the 1ft 11½in gauge Vale of Rheidol Light Railway was opened to traffic. In the 11 miles from Aberystwyth to Devil's Bridge the line climbs 680ft, 480ft of this being achieved on a gradient of 1 in 50 over the last four miles from Aberffrwd. As might be imagined, the route sticks closely to the contours in a way that no standard gauge line ever could, demonstrating the constructional value of building narrow gauge lines in mountainous districts.

To work alongside Rheidol, the company purchased the contractor's two ex-Plynlimon & Hafan Tramway Bagnall 2-6-2T locomotives built to its requirements by Davies & Metcalfe of Romiley. The railway traded with a modicum of success, small profits being made each year. In 1910 control of the line passed to nominated directors of the Cambrian Railways and in 1913 that company took over the Vale of Rheidol Railway.

The Cambrian was then itself absorbed by the Great Western Railway in 1923 and a review of services was undertaken. Two locomotives were built at Swindon to a design based on that of Davies & Metcalfe in 1923 and in 1924 a third was constructed using the spare parts made the previous year for the first two. One of the Davies & Metcalfe locomotives was scrapped in 1924, the second meeting the same fate in 1935.

Further activities under GWR ownership included closing the Harbour Branch and moving the Aberystwyth terminus to a site alongside the main line station in 1924. By the end of the 1920s the goods traffic had gone completely and in 1931 the winter service was withdrawn. The Vale of Rheidol Light Railway had become solely a tourist line.

In 1939 the line was closed for the duration of World War 2. Services were resumed in 1945, a prompt restoration being aided by the occasional maintenance given to the stock and track during the closure.

Below: **Probably bought by the Vale of Rheidol Light Railway Co as a shunter,** *Rheidol* **had a very active life until 1923, being the only locomotive allowed on the harbour branch but also working light trains to Devil's Bridge. It was scrapped at Swindon in 1924. The photograph shows it as first delivered at Aberystwyth.** *Loco Pub Co*

77697. ABERYSTWYTH, RHEIDOL VALLEY.

Above: **Whilst the V of R always recognised that a good proportion of its traffic would come from tourism, it also hoped to make good money from freight, which ambition was not fulfilled. A mixed train is seen at Rheidol Falls Halt in the 1920s. The (empty) wagons are lettered GW.** *Frith/commercial postcard*

Below: **GWR No 1213 was supposed to have been rebuilt at Swindon in 1924 but it was actually a new locomotive, identical to Nos 7 and 8, built in 1923, now known as No 9. It is seen approaching Devil's Bridge on 31 August 1937.** *R. E. Tustin*

The Aberystwyth terminus was abandoned in 1968 and the line diverted to a new location in the former Carmarthen line bay of the main line station. At the same time a new home for the stock was found in the standard gauge locomotive shed.

Restrictions on operation during the high fire-risk period of the dry summer of 1976 led to oil firing being adopted, No 7 being converted first. Both materials and advice were obtained from Boston Lodge, the Festiniog Railway's fleet having already been converted for similar reasons. The work was carried out in the shed at Aberystwyth, the first of a number of major tasks which have been undertaken there.

In August 1988 it was announced that the Rheidol was to be sold to the Brecon Mountain Railway for £306,500. The new owner commenced operations on 21 May 1989, with the same service as had been operated by BR. Locomotive No 9 was quickly transferred to Pant, the Brecon Mountain headquarters in South Wales, for a major overhaul. Since the change of ownership the passing loop at Aberffrwd has been reinstated, the timber Rheidol river bridge replaced and major work carried out on the locomotives and rolling stock, including the fitting of air brakes to replace the worn-out vacuum installations.

Above: **No 8 takes water at Aberffrwd in early BR days. Seen still in GW livery in 1953, the locomotive is now plain black and the carriages red and cream.** *P. B. Whitehouse*

Left: **By contrast, in July 1955 the BR lion and wheel crest has been applied.** *Real Photos*

Above right: **No 7 Owain Glyndwr passes Llanbadarn with the 2.45pm from Aberystwyth on 17 July 1963.** *P. J. Lynch*

Right: **Passengers wait for No 9 Prince of Wales at Nanyronen in the late 1950s.** *P. B. Whitehouse*

Left: **The Rheidol locomotives were named to launch the 1956 season. No 7 is seen with its crew posing for the publicity picture.** *British Railways (Western Region)*

Centre left: **No 8** *Llwelyn* **approaches Nantyronen on 20 August 1963.** *M. Dunnett*

Below: **A general view of Devil's Bridge with No 8 on the train in July 1955. A van and two wagons stand in the siding; the building to the left of them was the goods shed.** *Real Photos*

Above right: **With the second British Railways crest now applied, No 9 stands at Devil's Bridge in June 1963.** *Real Photos*

Below right: **In 1964 the Rheidol carriages were repainted in the livery shown here, dark green with gold lettering. The train was posed for publicity photographs; the livery lasted only a short time before being replaced by rail blue.** *British Railways (London Midland Region)*

Welsh Highland Railway

The Welsh Highland Railway grew out of the Croesor Tramway, a horse tramway which gave the Croesor Valley slate quarries access to Porthmadog; the North Wales Narrow Gauge Railways, a railway with a main line between Dinas Junction, near Caernarfon, and South Snowdon and a branch to Bryngwyn; and the Portmadoc, Beddgelert & South Snowdon Railway, a company which had powers to connect the NWNGR to the Croesor Tramway, via Beddgelert and the Aberglaslyn Pass, and to upgrade part of the Croesor and electrify the entire 21-mile route. The remains of the incomplete and abandoned PB&SSR construction around Beddgelert may still be seen; these lines were 1ft 11½in gauge. In 1922 the Welsh Highland Railway was created to take over the NWNGR, which had been moribund since 1916, and the PB&SSR, which had ceased trading in 1919, to restore and complete them as appropriate. The electrification plans were abandoned, resulting in a new route suitable for steam locomotives being constructed around Beddgelert. Allied with this development was the Festiniog Railway link with the WHR at Porthmadog. The complete railway was opened in 1923.

The Welsh Highland Railway owned three steam locomotives: *Moel Tryfan*, a NWNGR 0-6-4T single Fairlie built by Vulcan Foundry in 1875 but since 1917 incorporating the frames of the identical *Snowdon Ranger*; *Russell*, a Hunslet 2-6-2T built for the PB&SSR in 1906; and an ex-War Department Baldwin 4-6-0PT, No 590, built in 1917. The WHR's coaching stock was the surviving NWNGR fleet of 11 bogie vehicles. The FR link enabled through services to run from Blaenau Ffestiniog to Dinas.

Losses made each year resulted in a receiver being appointed in 1927. When no financial improvement was found to be possible during the following six years the line was closed. In the next year, 1934, it was reopened by the FR under the terms of a 42-year lease. Despite attempts to increase traffic, the FR could do no better and it was decided not to operate the line from 1937. The Welsh Highland Railway was then abandoned to the elements.

In 1941 the track between Dinas and Croesor Junction was, with other material and equipment, requisitioned to aid the war effort. The remainder was left in case the Croesor quarries reopened when hostilities ceased. They did not, so most of the remaining track, including that of the Croesor Tramway, was lifted by 1950.

The scheme to revive the Welsh Highland Railway began in 1961, with the formation of a society, later incorporated as the Welsh Highland Light Railway (1964) Ltd, a company limited by guarantee. The only surviving WHR locomotive, *Russell*, was donated to the company in 1965.

In 1973 the company gained access to the Beddgelert exchange siding, at Porthmadog, and alongside the WHR trackbed and the British Rail Cambrian Coast line, on which it has built a ¾-mile-long railway.

Public services commenced on 2 August 1980, with steam used for the first time on 30 April 1983. *Russell* worked its first passenger trains on 4 April 1987. The following year it returned triumphantly to the Festiniog Railway, where it

Left: **In October 1923 the press discovered the new railway. *Russell* is as built for the Portmadoc, Beddgelert & South Snowdon Railway in 1906, complete with air brakes.** *Topical Press*

ran passenger trains between Porthmadog and Rhiw Goch as part of the FR's 125th Anniversary of Steam celebrations.

In 1994, following a public inquiry the previous year, the Festiniog Railway was granted powers to acquire the Welsh Highland Railway trackbed. The FR intends to develop the line from the Caernarfon end, including the three-mile former standard gauge route between Caernarfon and Dinas Junction in its proposals. Two South African 'NGG16' class Garratts have been ordered for use on the line, with delivery expected early in 1996.

Above: **Porthmadog New, the Welsh Highland Railway's terminal in 1923, with trains crossing; the line crossed the GWR behind the trains. The field on which the station buildings stood, left, remained in Festiniog Railway ownership until the 1980s.** *Real Photos*

Below: **When the Welsh Highland first opened one of the features of its connection with the FR was the sight of steam trains running in the street.** *Author's collection*

Left: **Crossing the GWR proved to be an expense WHR traffic levels couldn't sustain so from 1931 trains stopped short of the crossing and passengers had to go across on foot.** *Russell*, **badly cut down to fit the Festiniog's loading gauge, is seen in 1934.** *Real Photos*

Below: **The Welsh Highland's Baldwin 4-6-0 No 590 was War Department surplus bought in 1923. It is arriving at Harbour station and will return to Dinas, it being too big for the FR.** *Author's collection*

Left: **The Festiniog Railway's** *Palmerston* **passes Waenfawr, on the North Wales Narrow Gauge Railway. The England engines' suitability for work on the Welsh Highland probably extended the life of more than one of them.** *Real Photos*

Welshpool & Llanfair Light Railway

Attempts to build a railway to serve Llanfair Caereinion, a small town about eight miles to the west of Welshpool, were first made in 1864 but it was 1903 before the 2ft 6in gauge railway eventually constructed was opened to traffic. Using powers obtained under the 1896 Light Railway legislation, the Welshpool & Llanfair Light Railway Co was able to persuade its larger standard gauge neighbour, the Cambrian Railways, to build and operate its line, with construction work starting in May 1901.

The railway was built to serve local agriculture, the only mineral traffic being incoming coal. To work its traffic the railway was provided with two Beyer Peacock 0-6-0T locomotives, named *The Earl* and *The Countess* after The Earl and Countess of Powis — The Earl had given land for the railway and was a director and shareholder.

The railway was not the success its promoters had forecast and it was never to pay a dividend to its shareholders. Small operating surpluses were sometimes made but these went to pay interest on loans. The 1922 Grouping of railways saw both the Cambrian and the Welshpool & Llanfair Railways being absorbed into the Great Western Railway.

Below: **A train of loaded cattle vans *en route* for Welshpool market with No 823 *Countess* in charge near Raven Square, c1950.** *P. B. Whitehouse*

Bottom: **In the 1920s *Countess* waits for time with a mixed train at Welshpool in 1929.** *W. H. Whitworth/Real Photos*

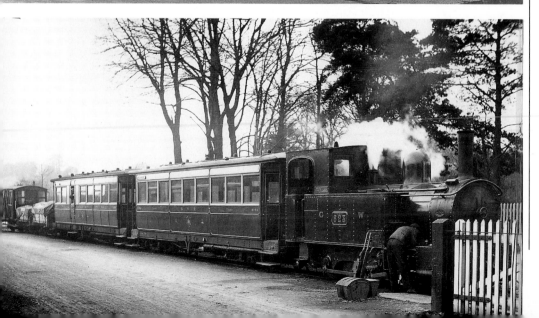

The passenger service was withdrawn in 1931. Towards the end of the 1930s the railway settled into an operating routine which was to continue into the 1950s. There was one return working most days, leaving Welshpool at 11am and arriving back at about 4pm. Upon Nationalisation in 1948 the line became a part of the Western Region; the last train ran on 2 November 1956.

The Welshpool & Llanfair Railway Preservation Society was established in 1956 and commenced negotiating with the British Transport Commission. By 1959 negotiations were sufficiently advanced for work to begin on clearing the undergrowth which was taking over the track. When sufficient clearance had been achieved, horses were hired to move the stock which the society was buying from British Railways. The details of a lease were agreed with the Transport Commission and the procedures for obtaining the necessary Light Railway Transfer Order were pursued. Meanwhile, a search for rolling stock was under way: passenger vehicles were obtained from a naval dockyard on the Medway, fortunately of the same gauge, and an appeal for funds to purchase the steam engines was put in hand.

The first passenger train run by the new management at Christmas 1962 was also the first public service for 31 years. The official reopening took place on 6 April 1963. The trains which ran that day also traversed the line through the town; by August the Council had completed its purchase of this section and had closed it for good. Welshpool had lost something which made both town and railway unique. Some relics remain, including some mixed gauge track set in concrete in the standard gauge yard.

The first regular trains ran from Llanfair Caereinion to Castle Caereinion — a distance of 4½ miles. From 1964 services were extended a further mile to Sylfaen. Concern about the state of the track on this section, coupled with the inability of the small track gang to cope with the additional workload, was the reason for re-terminating services at Castle Caereinion before the end of the season.

The search for additional locomotives and rolling stock continued. The articulated Bagnall 0-4-4-0T, *Monarch*, was obtained from Bowaters at Sittingbourne, Kent, in 1966. A friendship struck up with the similarly-gauged Zillertalbahn in the Austrian Tyrol resulted in four four-wheeled coaches being given to the railway in 1968. A Franco-Belge 0-8-0T locomotive, built in France to a German design for the German forces in 1944, was acquired from the Steiermärkische Landesbahnen, Austria, in 1969 and is now named *Sir Drefaldwyn* (Montgomeryshire).

The resulting operation of a continental train proved to be a major attraction and gave the company and its members ideas for further acquisitions. Suitable locomotives were to be subsequently obtained from Antigua, Sierra Leone and Finland. Sierra Leone was also the source of four modern bogie coaches.

As the railway became established and consolidated its position it was able to devote time to extending further, running to Sylfaen from 1972. The purchase of the freehold from British Rail in 1974 provided the impetus to complete the line back to Welshpool, achieved in July 1981.

Below left: **No 822** *The Earl* **had been thoroughly Swindonised by the time this photograph was taken at Welshpool's cattle market.** *Real Photos*

Above: **Both W&L locos photographed outside the shed at Welshpool. They have Swindon safety valve bonnets and original stovepipe chimneys.** *Real Photos*

Below: **On 25 March 1947** *The Earl* **was captured passing through Seven Stars with a mixed goods.** *R. E. Tustin*

Top: **A distinguishing feature of the Welshpool & Llanfair Light Railway was the Church Street crossing. No 822, with name plates removed, is seen on 12 October 1951.**
F. W. Shuttleworth

Above: **Passing Heniarth Station on 12 October 1951.**
F. W. Shuttleworth

Top: **The Countess** near Castle Caereinion with the ex-Admiralty stock in 1964. *Norman Gurley*

Above: **Shunting at Llanfair Caereinion before returning to Welshpool. An industrial estate has been built on the field behind the train.** *F. W. Shuttleworth*

125

Below: **The roadside station at Sylfaen was the terminus of the revived W&L for most of the 1964 season, before concern for the state of the track between there and Castle** Caereinion caused services to be cut back to the latter point. *The Countess* **was photographed at Sylfaen on 22 August that year.** *R. E. Tustin*

Bottom: ***The Earl*** **leaves Cyfronydd with the 2.55pm from Castle Caereinion on 13 April 1968.** *Allan Stewart*

Right: **The collapse of the Banwy bridge in December 1964 nearly brought the railway to grief. It is seen earlier that year with a train hauled by** *The Earl.* *Norman Gurley*

Below right: **Scenes like this one across the river near Llanfair Caereinion are no longer possible due to the development of the undergrowth. This was taken on 20 July 1968; the Zillertalbahn coach was one of three which had arrived on the railway in April that year.** *Allan Stewart*

BIBLIOGRAPHY

Andrews, John F., *The Story of Solomon Andrews & His Family*; Stewart Williams, 1976

Austin, Stephen, *From the Footplate — Cambrian Coast Express*; Ian Allan Ltd, 1992

Awdry, Christopher, *Encyclopaedia of British Railway Companies*; Patrick Stephens Ltd, 1990

Baughan, Peter E., *A Regional History of the Railways of Great Britain*, Volume XI: North and Mid Wales; David & Charles, 2nd edition 1991

Baughan, Peter E., *The Chester & Holyhead Railway*; David & Charles, 1972

Baughan, Peter E., *The North Wales Coast Railway — The Chester–Holyhead Line & Llandudno–Blaenau Ffestiniog*; Martin Bairstow, 1988

Boyd, J. I. C., *The Festiniog Railway* (2 vols); Oakwood Press, 1975

Boyd, J. I. C., *Narrow Gauge Railways in Mid-Wales*; Oakwood Press, 2nd edition 1970

Boyd, J. I. C., *Narrow Gauge Railways in South Caernarvonshire* (2 vols); Oakwood Press, 1988/9

Boyd, J. I. C., *Narrow Gauge Railways in North Caernarvonshire* (3 vols); Oakwood Press, 1980,1985/6

Boyd, J. I. C., *The Talyllyn Railway*; Wild Swan, 1988

Briwnant-Jones, G., *Railway through Talerddig*; Gomer, 1990

Cartwright, Ralph & Russell, R. T., *The Welshpool & Llanfair Light Railway*; David & Charles, 3rd edition 1989

Christiansen, R., *Forgotten Railways North and Mid Wales*; David & Charles, 2nd edition 1984

Christiansen, R. & Miller, R. W., *The Cambrian Railways* (2 vols); David & Charles, 1967 and 1968

Cox, David & Krupa, Christopher, *The Kerry Tramway and other Timber Light Railways*; Plateway Press, 1992

Cozens, Lewis, *The Mawddwy, Van and Kerry Railways*; Oakwood Press, 1972

Dalton, T. P., *Cambrian Companionship*; Oxford Publishing Co

Dow G.,: *'Midland at Machynlleth'*, Steam at Llangollen, Vol 1 No 1

Gasquoine, C. P., *The Story of the Cambrian*; Woodhall, Minshall, Thomas & Co, 1922

Goodall, Stephen P., *The Prestatyn and Dyserth Branch Line*; Oakwood Press, 1986

Green, C. C., *Cambrian Railways Album*; Ian Allan Ltd, 1977

Green, C. C., *Cambrian Railways Album 2*; Ian Allan Ltd, 1981

Green, C. C., *North Wales Branch Line Album*; Ian Allan Ltd, 1983

Green, C. C., *The Coast Lines of the Cambrian Railways Vol 1*; Wild Swan, 1993

Green, C. C., *The Vale of Rheidol Railway*; Wild Swan, 1986

Hambly, Mark & Southern, Dave, *Railways of the Dee Valley*; Llangollen Railway Society, 1989

Huntriss, Derek, *On Cambrian Lines*; Ian Allan Ltd, 1993

Johnson, Peter, *Portrait of the Festiniog*; Ian Allan Ltd, 1992

Johnson, Peter, *Rails in Wales — The Cambrian Lines*; Ian Allan Ltd, 1984

Johnson, Peter, *The Welsh Narrow Gauge in Colour*; Ian Allan Ltd, 1993

Kennedy, Rex, *Steam on the Cambrian*; Ian Allan Ltd, 1990

Kidner, R. W., *The Cambrian Railways*; Oakwood Press, revised edition 1992

Lloyd, Mike, *The Tanat Valley Light Railway*; Wild Swan; 1990

Magner, C. (Ed.), *Wales Rail: A route guide to the scenic rail routes of Wales*; Cambrian Coast Line Action Group, 198

Magner, C. (Ed.), *Cambrian Rail: British Rail scenic rail routes in mid Wales*; Cambrian Coast Line Action Group & Vale of Rheidol Railway Supporters Association, 1982

Magner, C. (Ed.), *Great Wales Rail: A route guide to the scenic rail routes of mid Wales*; Cambrian Coast Line Action Group, 1983

Milner, W. J., *The Glyn Valley Tramway*; Oxford Publishing Co, 1984

Morgan, John Scott, *Corris: A Narrow Gauge Portrait*; Irwell Press, 1991

Ottley, George, *A Bibliography of British Railway History*; HMSO, 2nd edition 1983

Prideaux, J., *The Welsh Narrow Gauge Railway: A pictorial history*; David & Charles, 1976

Rear, W. G. & Williams, M. F., *The Cambrian Coast Railway*; Foxline Publishing, 1988

Rear, W. G. & Williams, M. F., *The Conwy Valley Line: Blaenau Ffestiniog to Llandudno Junction*; Foxline Publishing, 1991

Rear, W. G. & Williams, M. F., *The Llangollen Line: Ruabon to Barmouth*; Foxline Publishing, 1990

Southern, D. W., Leadbetter, H. J. & Weatherley, S. A., *Rails to Bala*; Charter Publications, 1987

Thompson, Trefor, *Railways of North Wales: The Modern Era*; T. & M. Thompson, 1982

Turner, Keith, *The Snowdon Mountain Railway*; David & Charles, 1973

Turner, Keith, *North Wales Tramways*; David & Charles, 1979

Turner, Susan, *The Padarn & Penrhyn Railways*; David & Charles, 1975

Williams, G. Haulfryn, *Railways in Gwynedd*; Gwynedd Archives Service, 1979

Williams, Herbert, *Davies, the Ocean Railway King and Coal Tycoon*; University of Wales Press, 1991

Wirral Railway Circle, *Cambrian Coast Express: An illustrated route description and history of the Cambrian Rail routes and associated lines*; WRC, 1973

Wirral Railway Circle, *North Wales Land Cruise*; WRC, 1976

Wren, Wilfred, J., *The Tanat Valley Light Railway*; Oakwood Press, 1979